Business

for Cambridge IGCSE™ and O Level

WORKBOOK

Alex Smith & Veenu Jain

Second edition with Digital access

Shaftesbury Road, Cambridge CB2 8EA, United Kingdom

One Liberty Plaza, 20th Floor, New York, NY 10006, USA

477 Williamstown Road, Port Melbourne, VIC 3207, Australia

314–321, 3rd Floor, Plot 3, Splendor Forum, Jasola District Centre, New Delhi – 110025, India

103 Penang Road, #05–06/07, Visioncrest Commercial, Singapore 238467

Cambridge University Press & Assessment is a department of the University of Cambridge.

We share the University's mission to contribute to society through the pursuit of education, learning and research at the highest international levels of excellence.

www.cambridge.org
Information on this title: www.cambridge.org/9781009813549

© Cambridge University Press & Assessment 2025

This publication is in copyright. Subject to statutory exception and to the provisions of relevant collective licensing agreements, no reproduction of any part may take place without the written permission of Cambridge University Press & Assessment.

First published 2019
Second edition 2025
20 19 18 17 16 15 14 13 12 11 10 9 8 7 6 5 4 3 2 1

Printed in Malaysia by Vivar Printing

A catalogue record for this publication is available from the British Library

ISBN 978-1-009-81354-9 Workbook

Additional resources for this publication at www.cambridge.org/9781009813549

Cambridge University Press & Assessment has no responsibility for the persistence or accuracy of URLs for external or third-party internet websites referred to in this publication and does not guarantee that any content on such websites is, or will remain, accurate or appropriate. Third-party websites and resources referred to in this publication are not endorsed.

Cambridge International Education material in this publication is reproduced under licence and remains the intellectual property of Cambridge University Press & Assessment.

The Cambridge Pathway offers five stages of education from age 3 to 19, with curriculum, resources and assessment. Registered Cambridge International Schools benefit from high-quality programmes, qualifications, assessments and a wide range of support so that teachers can effectively deliver in the classroom. Visit www.cambridgeinternational.org to find out more.

For EU product safety concerns, contact us at Calle de José Abascal, 56, 1°, 28003 Madrid, Spain, or email eugpsr@cambridge.org.

> Endorsement

Endorsement indicates that a resource has passed Cambridge International Education's rigorous quality-assurance process and is suitable to support the delivery of their syllabus. However, endorsed resources are not the only suitable materials available to support teaching and learning, and are not essential to achieve the qualification. For the full list of endorsed resources to support this syllabus, visit www.cambridgeinternational.org/endorsed-resources

Any example answers to questions taken from past question papers, practice questions, accompanying marks and mark schemes included in this resource have been written by the authors and are for guidance only. They do not replicate examination papers. In examinations, the way marks are awarded may be different. Any references to assessment and/or assessment preparation are the publisher's interpretation of the syllabus requirements. Examiners will not use endorsed resources as a source of material for any assessment set by Cambridge International Education.

While the publishers have made every attempt to ensure that advice on the qualification and its assessment is accurate, the official syllabus, specimen assessment materials and any associated assessment guidance materials produced by the awarding body are the only authoritative source of information and should always be referred to for definitive guidance.

Our approach is to provide teachers with access to a wide range of high-quality resources that suit different styles and types of teaching and learning.

For more information about the endorsement process, please visit www.cambridgeinternational.org/endorsed-resources.

2024 Cambridge Dedicated Teacher Awards

Our **Cambridge Dedicated Teacher Awards** are an opportunity to show appreciation for the incredible work teachers do every day.

Thank you to everyone who nominated this year; we have been inspired and moved by all of your stories. Well done to all of our nominees for your dedication to learning and for inspiring the next generation of thinkers, leaders and innovators.

Congratulations to our winners!

Global Winner
South East Asia & Pacific
Sydney Engelbert
Keningau Vocational College, Malaysia

East Asia
Pengfei Jiang
Zhuji Ronghuai Foreign Language School, China

Pakistan
Saeeda Salim
SISA - School of International Studies in Sciences & Arts, Pakistan

South Asia
Meena Mishra
Dr Sarvepalli Radhakrishnan International School, India

Middle East and North Africa
Gina Justus
Our Own English High school- Sharjah- Girls, United Arab Emirates

Sub-Saharan Africa
Tajudeen Odufeso
Isara Secondary School, Isara Remo, Nigeria

Europe
Aynur Bayazit
Menekşe Ahmet Yalçınkaya Kindergarten, Türkiye

Latin America & the Caribbean
Ramon Majé Floriano
Montessori sede San Francisco, Colombia

North America
Marisa Santos
Seminole Ridge Community High School, United States

For more information about our dedicated teachers and their stories, go to dedicatedteacher.cambridge.org

Contents

How to use this series ... vi
How to use this book ... vii
Introduction ... viii
Developing skills for business ... x

1 **Understanding business activity** ... 1
　1　Business activity ... 2
　2　Economic sectors ... 6
　3　Enterprise, business growth and size ... 11
　4　Types of business organisations ... 18
　5　Business objectives and stakeholder objectives ... 24
　Section 1 Practice questions ... 29

2 **People in business** ... 35
　6　Human resource management ... 36
　7　Organisation and management ... 43
　8　Methods of communication ... 51
　9　Motivating employees ... 59
　Section 2 Practice questions ... 67

3 **Marketing** ... 73
　10　Marketing and the market ... 74
　11　Market research ... 81
　12　Marketing mix: product ... 87
　13　Marketing mix: price ... 91
　14　Marketing mix: place ... 95
　15　Marketing mix: promotion ... 98
　16　Marketing strategy and legal controls ... 103
　Section 3 Practice questions ... 109

4 **Operations management** ... 115
　17　Production of goods and services ... 116
　18　Costs, scale of production and break-even analysis ... 125
　19　Quality of goods and services ... 132
　20　Location decisions ... 138
　Section 4 Practice questions ... 143

5 **Financial information and decisions** ... 149
　21　Business finance ... 150
　22　Cash flow forecasts ... 156
　23　Statement of profit or loss ... 162
　24　Statement of financial position ... 168
　25　Analysis of accounts ... 174
　Section 5 Practice questions ... 182

6 **External influences on business activity** ... 189
　26　Economic issues ... 190
　27　Business and the international economy ... 197
　28　Environmental and ethical issues ... 202
　Section 6 Practice questions ... 208

Acknowledgements ... 213

BUSINESS FOR CAMBRIDGE IGCSE™ AND O LEVEL: WORKBOOK

> How to use this series

All the components in the series are designed to work together.

The coursebook is designed for students to use in class with guidance from the teacher. It supports the *Cambridge IGCSE™, IGCSE 1–9 and O Level Business* syllabuses (0264/0774/7081). The coursebook is split into six sections and contains in-depth explanations of business concepts, a variety of independent and group activities, interesting case studies to engage students and help them make real-world connections.

A digital version of the coursebook is included with the print version and is also available separately. It includes access to video case studies as well as simple tools for students to use in class or for self-study.

The workbook provides further practice of all the skills presented in the coursebook and is ideal for use in class or as homework. It provides engaging activities, worked examples and opportunities for students to evaluate sample answers so they can put into practice what they have learnt.

A digital version of the workbook is included with the print version. It includes simple tools for students to use in class or for self-study.

The digital teacher's resource provides everything teachers need to deliver this course. It is packed full of useful teaching notes and lesson ideas, with suggestions for differentiation to support and challenge students, ideas for formative assessment and overcoming common misconceptions, and language support.

The digital teacher's resource also contains downloadable worksheets.

All answers to coursebook and workbook activities are available to teachers via Cambridge GO.

> How to use this book

Throughout this workbook, you will notice recurring features that are designed to help your learning. Here is a brief overview of what you will find.

> **LEARNING INTENTIONS**
>
> Learning intentions open each chapter. These help you with navigation through the workbook and indicate the important concepts in each topic. The learning intentions also map to the content in the *Business for Cambridge IGCSE™ and O level Coursebook*.

> **KEY TERMS**
>
> These provide a reminder of the key terms that you need to recall for each chapter topic.

Activities

These are scaffolded exercises that support your progression through your course and enable you to put into practice what you have learnt up to that point. The activities have been clearly linked to the key skills that you need for business.

> **REFLECTION**
>
> Reflections enable you to look back on your work and encourage you to think about your learning. You will reflect on and assess the process that you used to arrive at your answers.

> **TIPS**
>
> Tips are provided throughout this workbook to help with your learning. These provide you with additional guidance and advice.

End-of-section practice questions

More demanding practice questions provide you with an opportunity to try out further questions on what you have learnt in each section. The answers to these questions should be completed in your own notebook.

> **WORKED EXAMPLES**
>
> Worked examples provide you with sample answers in order to help you understand how to respond to questions using key skills. The answers are annotated with an abbreviated version of the relevant key skills:
>
> - [K] Knowledge and understanding
> - [Ap] Application
> - [An] Analysis
> - [E] Evaluation

Improve this answer

This offers you an opportunity to evaluate a sample answer to a question.

Your challenge

You are provided with advice and guidance on ehow the answer could be improved and then asked to apply this advice to write your own improved answer.

> Introduction

This workbook is designed to help you develop your skills in Cambridge IGCSE™ and O Level Business and to improve your learning of the course material. A key part of this is developing your skills in the way you answer business-related questions.

Developing skills for business

The first section goes through each aspect of what it takes to effectively show your knowledge of business studies. To do this, it goes through the following areas:

- the use of command words in questions
- how to apply your analytical and evaluative skills to business scenarios
- answering questions using business data, charts and numbers
- improving your skills through reflective learning.

How the activities are structured

Each section of the workbook focuses on the different business topics followed in the coursebook. The book is structured to help you in the following ways.

Use of stimulus material

As you progress through your course, you will become familiar with answering questions in the form of short case scenarios. These questions are designed to help you practise applying key business skills to realistic business scenarios. It is important that you remember to refer to the information in the case scenarios to support your answers to questions.

Supporting guidance on activities

Many of the questions at the beginning of the workbook offer support and guidance designed to help you better understand particular question types and also build your skills. As you progress through the workbook and become more confident in answering business studies questions, the amount of guidance will be reduced. Each section also includes helpful tips to improve your question technique.

Importance of reflection

A key part of learning how to develop your business studies skills is through reflection. At the end of each chapter, there is a guide to aspects you can reflect on based on the learning themes. When you are doing the activities, however, you should be continuously reflecting on the whole learning process and asking yourself how you can improve your answers.

Introduction

Practice questions

At the end of each section you will find a series of practice questions, including short answer, data response and case study questions. The authors have written a selection of sample answers to the practice questions, with suggestions about how they could be improved. Here, you will have the opportunity to apply your own skills in order to think about and write a better answer in each case.

Online answers

There are online answers to each activity. An effective way to improve your learning is to answer the questions and use the answers to reflect on how well your business skills are developing.

The aim of this book is to develop and support your learning in business. Many of the activities put you in the position of a business owner who is looking at a business and has to assess the issues and challenges that the business faces when making decisions. The questions test your knowledge and understanding of business but also give you the opportunity to think like a business owner and make the judgements needed for effective decision-making.

> Developing skills for business

What is expected from your answers to questions?

Throughout this book, you are going to answer questions that develop and improve your business skills. There are two key things to focus on:

- What makes an 'excellent answer'?
- How can you learn the skills needed to produce 'excellent answers'?

This section of the book looks at the areas that you will need to concentrate on to make your business skills as good as they can be.

The importance of command words in questions

The skills that you will need to show will differ, depending on the command words used in different questions. A command word is a term or phrase that appears in a question that is asking you to show a particular skill. The command words that you will become familiar with during your business course are:

- 'State' – to set out an idea, term or point in a few words.
  State the break-even output of a business's new project.

- 'Calculate' – to work out a value from set facts and figures.
  Calculate the value of ABC's gross profit from Table 1.1.

- 'Define' – to give the precise meaning of a term.
  Define 'labour turnover'.

- 'Identify' – to name or select an idea, term or point.
  Identify **four** stages in the recruitment and selection process.

- 'Outline' – to set out the main points.
  Outline **two** sources of external finance that XYZ might use for the new factory.

- 'Explain' – to establish relationships and reasons why and how things happen.
  Explain **two** reasons why branding might be important to XYZ.

- 'Justify' – to make a reasoned argument that is supported by evidence.
  Do you think that XYZ should expand its market by entering a new market in another country? Justify your answer.

- 'Consider' – evaluate the information you have been provided with.
  Consider whether you think Sani is right to relocate her business operation to Country X.

Developing skills for business

There are specific areas of knowledge and skills that you will learn while studying business, and this workbook contains questions that will help you to develop and practise these skills, including:

- knowledge and understanding of business facts and theory
- application of business facts and theory
- analytical skills in the way you use evidence and reason
- evaluative skills by making judgements and recommendations.

You will not be expected to show all of these skills at the same time, but the different questions will develop these skills in stages as you move through a whole question.

The workbook contains practice questions at the end of each section, which have been written by the authors. You will find sample answers (also written by the authors) for you to work on improving, which will help you to practise how to further develop your skills.

Knowledge and understanding

You will need to show an accurate knowledge and understanding of all the concepts you have studied during your course. All types of question are designed to help check your knowledge and understanding, but knowledge-based questions usually use the command words 'identify' and 'state'. Here is an example of how you might need to show your knowledge and understanding. Look at the sample answer given and decide what you might do to improve it before reading on:

Q Identify **four** external stakeholder groups a business might have.

....

....

....

.... [4]

Have a go at this question and then compare your response to this sample answer. How does your answer compare?

Government, local community, customers and suppliers.

BUSINESS FOR CAMBRIDGE IGCSE™ AND O LEVEL: WORKBOOK

Application

To answer questions effectively, you need to apply your knowledge and understanding of business facts, ideas and theory to business situations. This means answering clearly and accurately by using the case study material. This is crucial in answering all types of questions. Here is an example of a question that uses the 'outline' command word:

Q Outline **two** sources of finance ABC Farm might use to buy a new piece of equipment.

....

....

....

.... **[4]**

Have a go at this question and then compare your response to this sample answer. How does your answer compare?

ABC Farm could use retained profits from previous years. This is profit made each year by the farm and can be used to buy the new equipment. It could also lease the machinery from a finance company. ABC Farm pays a sum of money each month to a finance company to pay for a new tractor but does not actually own the tractor.

Analysis

Analysis is a crucial skill that you need to develop in business, and questions where you need to show this skill often contain the command word 'explain', or 'justify'.
This means making a point and then making links to how and why something happens. Consider this question, for example:

Imagine the following scenario: CGB is a toy manufacturer that uses flow production. The factory has 80 skilled employees. The Human Resources Manager is concerned that many employees are leaving and is considering ways to increase employee motivation.

Q Explain **two** ways CGB's managers could improve employee motivation.

....

....

....

....

....

.... **[6]**

Developing skills for business

Have a go at this question and then compare your response to this sample answer. How does your answer compare?

The manager could offer training to improve the skills of the 80 employees. Another method is job rotation, which would allow employees to switch between similar jobs in the factory so they do not get bored doing the same job all the time.

Evaluation

The ability to evaluate is a very important skill needed for business. Questions that use the command word 'justify' are looking for you to make judgements about the argument that you have developed in your answer. You will need to show effective knowledge and understanding, application, and analysis, but you will then need to build on this by making judgements about the points that you make. This can be done by:

- explaining the relative importance of the point you have made
- suggesting a weakness or opposing view
- considering how the argument developed could change over time
- questioning any assumptions that you have made.

This is an example of a question that requires evaluative skills:

Q Do you think the advantages to CGB of using flow production are greater than the disadvantages? Justify your answer.

....

....

....

....

....

.... [6]

Have a go at this question and then compare your response to this sample answer. How does your answer compare?

One advantage is economies of scale which can reduce CGB's average cost per unit. However, flow production is inflexible. Being difficult to change means the business may not be able to respond quickly to changes in customer demands.

I think the advantages are greater, as the lower average cost per unit could result in lower prices which can increase demand for toys. If the product has high sales this could reduce the need for flexibility.

Using stimulus and case study materials

All the questions in this workbook are based on stimulus material. In the main sections of the book, this appears in the form of short business scenarios that provide data and additional context for a particular question. In the practice questions, you will encounter stimulus material in both the practice questions and in the case studies located at the end of each section of the book.

The stimulus material and the questions in the book are designed to help you apply the knowledge and skills you have acquired during your course.

- For short answer and data response questions, you will be provided with a piece of stimulus material, which will take the form of a business scenario. It is important that you refer to these business scenarios and any supporting data in your answers.

- For case study questions, you may be presented with additional stimulus material in the form of appendices. You should remember to refer to any relevant data that may support your argument in your answers.

Using numbers and charts

Some of the questions that you answer will involve the use of data, diagrams, charts and calculations. Being able to use this type of information effectively is a very important business skill. The questions in the book that involve the use of numbers and charts will require you to:

- show knowledge and understanding of data used, for example, by showing your understanding of a pie chart that shows the market share of different businesses in an industry

- be able to apply data to a business situation, for example, explaining what a rise in cash inflow means for a business's liquidity

- be able to calculate a figure from a given set of data, such as using revenue and cost to calculate profit

- analyse data to explain business issues, such as what rising revenue figures tell us about the effectiveness of a marketing strategy

- evaluate the usefulness of data and make judgements. If, for example, the gross profit figure is falling, does it mean that the business is failing to control cost efficiently or is it caused by another factor such as falling prices?

This is a sample question and answer

The table shows the statement of profit or loss for SRT for the last year. SRT is a food manufacturer based in Country X. The business uses batch production in its factory. SRT has 600 employees, all of whom receive regular training.

	$m
Revenue	4
Cost of sales	2.2
Gross profit	1.8
Expenses	1.2
Profit	0.6

Have a go at this question and then compare your response to this sample answer. How does your answer compare? How would you improve the sample answer?

1   Calculate the profit margin for SRT. Show your working.

....

....

Profit margin = $\dfrac{\text{profit}}{\text{revenue}} \times 100$

Profit margin = 15%

2   Outline **two** ways SRT could increase profit.

....

....

....

....

Increase revenue by increasing the price of its food products. It could also try to lower fixed costs, for example, by reducing the amount of rent paid at its factory.

3   Explain **two** advantages to SRT of using batch production.

....

....

....

....

....

One advantage is that it offers flexibility, so if demand for one of its food products changes, SRT can quickly adapt production to meet the new level of demand. Also, if there is a problem with the machinery, the whole production line is not affected, which means the factory can still produce some output to fulfil some orders.

4 Explain **two** methods of training SRT could use. Which is the best method for SRT to use? Justify your answer.

....

....

....

....

....

....

....

SRT could use on-the-job training. This is a low-cost method of training for its 600 employees. SRT could also use off-the-job training, which allows employee to make mistakes when learning. Off-the-job training is better especially for a food manufacturer business because fewer mistakes can help protect the business reputation. This could lead to additional customers and the revenue gained from them could help towards paying the higher cost of using off-the-job training.

Improve your skills through reflective learning

At the end of each chapter in this book, there is a reflection that gets you to think about what you have learnt and how you could improve next time. If you follow the process of reflection throughout the book, your understanding of the subject will improve and you will write better answers to questions. Here is a reflective process you could use when you are doing the activities in this book:

- Complete one of the activities in the book.
- Review your answers and check them against the learning intentions.
- Compare your answer to the answers given online.
- Think of the areas in which you need to improve.
- Put the improvements that you have thought of into practice when you do the next activity.

Consider this example of the reflective process by completing the following sample question

ARC is a small retail business that sells mobile phone accessories. It has two shops. The business was started four years ago by Luis, who is operating as a sole trader. Luis uses a range of methods to promote his business. Luis is considering expanding ARC by opening another shop. This will require $10 000 finance. An investor has already approached Luis, offering the $10 000 in return for becoming a business partner.

Developing skills for business

1 Define 'sole trader'.

....

....

This is a business owned and controlled by one person who takes all the risks and all the profits.

REFLECTION
How did I use precise business terminology?

2 Outline **two** methods ARC might use to promote its products.

....

....

....

....

It could advertise its phone accessories on social media to raise awareness. It could also provide offers such as 'buy one get one free', which could tempt customers to visit the two shops.

REFLECTION
Where did I apply the case example clearly to support my answer?

3 Explain **two** advantages to ARC of expanding the business.

....

....

....

....

....

Sample answer: *Opening another shop would mean more customers, which could result in more revenue. Another advantage is it would help spread risk because ARC is not relying on customers in one location for their business. The sales gained from the new shop can make up for any potential loss in sales in the other two shops.*

> **REFLECTION**
>
> How am I making it clear why ARC's expansion will be beneficial to the business?

4 Do you think the advantages to Luis of taking a business partner are greater than the disadvantages? Justify your answer.

....

....

....

....

....

....

....

By taking finance from the investor, Luis would get the $10 000 he needs to grow his business. Having a partner would mean he would have someone to share the costs and risks with. It would, however, mean that he would lose some control over the business because he would then have to discuss decisions with a partner. This could be a problem if the new investor wanted to take ARC in a direction that Luis did not want. Luis would still have unlimited liability so he could risk losing his personal assets if the business fails. Remaining a sole trader is better because the business is already successful, so he may have the funds to expand, and the risk of giving up control may not be something that Luis wants or needs to do.

> **REFLECTION**
>
> How have I developed my argument to justify the conclusion I have come to?

Section 1
Understanding business activity

> Chapter 1
Business activity

LEARNING INTENTIONS

By the end of this chapter, you will be able to:

- define and provide examples of the four factors of production
- understand the importance of 'added value'
- explain ways a business can increase added value
- understand the concept of opportunity cost.

KEY TERMS

| added value | factors of production | opportunity cost |

Activity 1.1

This activity is designed to test your understanding of business activity.

Creations is a public limited company. It is a skiwear manufacturer whose business activity is to produce a range of clothing for skiers. The main target market is customers who buy clothing for skiing, but Creations also targets customers who buy ski clothing as leisure wear. The business has had a difficult year and has seen its sales fall by 10%.

1. State **two** needs involved in Creations' business activity.

   Reflect on the reasons why people need to buy clothing.

   ....

   ....

2. Outline the **two** wants involved in Creations' business activity.

   Consider the goods that you buy but do not actually need.

   ....

   ....

   ....

> **TIP**
>
> To outline, you will need to set out the main points in your answer by describing the want the skiwear is satisfying. Think about the reasons why people buy skiwear as a guide to the nature of wants.

1 Business activity

3 Explain **two** reasons why Creations might have experienced a decrease in sales in the last year. Which reason do you think is the most important to Creations? Justify your answer.

Here you could make a link between changes in wants/needs and Creations' sales when thinking about one of the reasons why sales might have decreased.

....

....

....

....

....

....

....

Activity 1.2

This activity tests your knowledge of the different factors of production.

A mobile phone manufacturer uses the following resources to produce and sell its mobile phones:

- land
- labour
- capital
- enterprise.

Identify the type of resource in each case by completing Table 1.1.

Table 1.1: Types of resources used in mobile phone manufacturing

Resource	Type
Components used in the mobile phones	
Workers in the marketing department	
Person who started the business	
Plastic used to make the screens for the mobile phones	
The firm's computer system	
Equipment used on the production line	
Individuals who own shares in the business	
Employees who work on the production line	

Activity 1.3

> **The aim of this activity is to test your understanding of opportunity costs.**

Faster Gym is a business that operates a chain of gyms in New Zealand. The business was set up by Christina and James five years ago after they finished their careers in athletics. Faster Gym is successful with memberships growing by 10% each year since the business was started. Christina and James believe in investing in the best and latest gym equipment and employing highly skilled staff to work in their gyms. Faster Gym wants to open a new gym in Auckland at a cost of $1.5 million, but this comes with an opportunity cost because the cost of the investment leaves less money to spend on new equipment for the existing gyms.

1   Define 'opportunity cost'.

    Be clear and precise with definition questions.

    ....

    ....

2   Outline the labour and capital resources used by Faster Gym.

    Think about the people who work in gyms and the type of equipment they use.

    ....

    ....

    ....

    ....

3   Explain **two** reasons Faster Gym's membership might have grown by 10% each year.

    Consider the reasons why more people would want to go to gyms.

    ....

    ....

    ....

    ....

    ....

    ....

1 Business activity

4 Do you think the advantages to Faster Gym of opening a new gym are greater than the disadvantages? Justify your answer.

Consider the advantages and disadvantages of Faster Gym opening a new gym. Make a decision as to whether you think it should open the new gym or not. Justify this decision.

....

....

....

....

....

....

....

....

....

....

....

....

....

....

REFLECTION

How well have you understood the different aspects of business activity? What have been the easiest parts and what have been the most difficult parts of this topic? Have your answers to the questions in this chapter helped your understanding? Try discussing your answers to the questions in this chapter with your teacher to improve your understanding.

Chapter 2
Economic sectors

> **LEARNING INTENTIONS**
>
> By the end of this chapter, you will be able to:
>
> - understand the purpose of the primary, secondary and tertiary sectors
> - explain the difference between the primary, secondary and tertiary sectors
> - understand the meaning and purpose of private and public sectors
> - explain the difference between private and public sectors.

> **KEY TERMS**
>
> primary sector   private sector   public sector
> secondary sector   tertiary sector

Activity 2.1

This activity is designed to check your understanding of the primary, secondary and tertiary sectors of the economy.

In Table 2.1, there is a list of goods and services that need to be matched with the business activity they are associated with.

Table 2.1: Goods or services to match the business activity with which they are associated

Good or service	Business activity (primary, secondary, tertiary)
School	
Manufacturing wind turbines	
Gym membership	
Microwave oven	
Music streaming service	
Rice growing	
Mobile phone	
Airline ticket	
Rare earth metal mining	

> **TIP**
>
> When you are choosing whether a good or service is primary, secondary or tertiary, think about how the good or service is produced.

Activity 2.2

> This activity will help you to check your understanding of how business operates in the private and public sectors.

In a town near Delhi, a local school owned and controlled by the government is the major employer in the area. Individuals contribute to various roles within the school, including teachers, administrative staff, caretakers and other support staff. Additionally, the school buys services from two private limited companies, one for cleaning services and another for catering.

1 Define 'public sector'.

   Write your definition precisely using exact terminology.

   ....

   ....

2 Outline **two** reasons why schools are often in the public sector.

   Try to focus clearly on the factors that make an organisation private or public sector.

   ....

   ....

   ....

   ....

3 Explain why the school and the businesses that service it are an example of organisations in a mixed economy.

   Show your analytical skills by making connections between the ownership of an organisation and the nature of the economy.

   ....

   ....

   ....

   ....

   ....

Activity 2.3

> This activity checks your knowledge and understanding of a public sector tertiary business.

Sintau Hospital is a government-financed hospital that is having difficulties improving patient care. The management of the hospital wants to improve its efficiency and manage the organisation more effectively. Sintau Hospital wants to focus on reducing waiting times.

1 State whether Sintau Hospital is in the primary, secondary, or tertiary sector.

   ....

2 Outline **two** characteristics of Sintau Hospital as a public sector organisation.

   It is important to think about what makes an organisation part of the public sector.

   ....

   ....

   ....

   ....

3 Explain why Sintau Hospital might find it difficult to reduce patient waiting times.

   Consider the pressures state-funded and state-managed organisations are under.

   ....

   ....

   ....

   ....

   ....

   ....

2 Economic sectors

Activity 2.4

This activity gets you to look at the aims and decision-making of a private sector tertiary business.

The fitness industry has experienced significant growth over the past decade. Large gym chains are now established in many towns and cities, accompanied by numerous independent fitness centres. Australian consumers have developed a taste for a variety of workout experiences, including strength training, cardio exercises and group fitness classes.

1   State **two** possible aims of the decisions made by businesses in the fitness industry.

   Think of all the aims that businesses might have in the private sector.

   ....

   ....

2   Outline how firms in the fitness market in Australia make private sector decisions in terms of what, how and for whom to produce goods and provide services.

   A strong answer would use an example of how resources are allocated through the gym market.

   ....

   ....

   ....

   ....

Activity 2.5

This activity aims to test your understanding of a market where there is some debate as to whether businesses should operate in the private sector or the public sector.

VNT Buses is a transportation company that runs buses in the southern region of Vietnam, operating in the tertiary sector of the economy. It is a private sector business with the objective of achieving an yearly profit of $150 million. Additionally, the company aims to boost its profit by 6% over the next three years. VNT Buses plans to achieve this by incorporating new technology and implementing cost-cutting measures. The potential for job redundancies to reduce operational costs has raised concerns among many of the employees at VNT Buses.

1   Define 'tertiary sector'.

   Write your definition precisely using exact terminology.

   ....

   ....

2   Outline **two** possible objectives of VNT as a private sector business.

   Think about the objectives that private sector businesses have to be successful.

   ....

   ....

   ....

   ....

REFLECTION

How well have you developed your knowledge and understanding in this topic? Think of ways you can improve this. Try completing the questions in this chapter and see how your answers have improved your knowledge and understanding over time.

> Chapter 3

Enterprise, business growth and size

LEARNING INTENTIONS

By the end of this chapter, you will be able to:

- explain the characteristics of successful entrepreneurs
- understand the key elements and importance of a business plan
- explain why and how governments support business start-ups
- know the methods and problems of measuring business size
- understand the reasons why some businesses grow and others remain small
- describe the different ways a business can grow, both internally and externally
- explain the advantages and disadvantages of different methods of growth
- understand the reasons why some businesses succeed and others fail.

KEY TERMS

| business plan | entrepreneur | horizontal integration |
| merger | takeover | vertical integration |

Activity 3.1

This activity aims to improve your knowledge of the characteristics of an entrepreneur.

Atchara wants to start a fashion business in Thailand. Complete Table 3.1 by matching these examples of how Atchara might show the characteristics of a social entrepreneur:

- wants to use social media in marketing
- has many contacts in the fashion business
- has used her house to secure a loan to start the business
- has arranged a loan to fully fund the business
- enjoys presenting her ideas to potential investors

- enjoys working long hours
- has set a target revenue of $4 million in the first three years of business
- is well respected in the local community for her honest business practices
- has a master's degree and professional qualification in architecture.

Think about some of the well-known entrepreneurs you know when considering the characteristics of entrepreneurs.

Table 3.1: The characteristics of entrepreneurs

Characteristic	Example
Innovative	
Self-motivated and determined	
Self-confident	
Multi-skilled	
Has strong leadership qualities	
Takes initiative	
Results-driven	
Risk-taker	
Good networker	

Activity 3.2

This activity helps to develop your understanding of what is in a business plan and how it might be useful to different stakeholders.

Adriana has recently left her position at a corporate office in Tokyo, and she is eager to start a new venture – opening a coffee shop in São Paulo. Adriana has seen an increasing demand for quality coffee experiences in the local market and she sees a promising opportunity to establish a thriving business. Adriana has started discussions with a bank to secure funding and they have asked for a business plan. Additionally, Adriana is exploring potential government support programs that could benefit new small businesses in the coffee market.

1 Identify **four** ways that the government could support Adriana's new business.

   You need to list four ways the government supports businesses.

   ....

   ....

   ....

   ....

3 Enterprise, business growth and size

2 Outline **two** reasons why a business plan might be useful to Adriana in her new business.

   Here you need to take an element of a business plan, such as sales and cost forecasts, and set out what might be produced.

   ....

   ....

   ....

   ....

3 Explain **two** reasons why it might be important for Adriana to have a business plan. Which reason do you think is the most important to Adriana? Justify your answer.

   Think about the importance of different elements of the plan and why this might be useful to Adriana.

   ....

   ....

   ....

   ....

   ....

   ....

   ....

   ....

Activity 3.3

This activity helps you to look at how the sizes of businesses are measured.

BrightElec S.A. is a large Brazilian electrical retailer, employing 20,000 workers and with a revenue of $0.9 billion. FoodConnect S.A., on the other hand, is a food manufacturing business with 35,000 employees and a revenue of $3.8 billion. FoodConnect S.A. received substantial support from the Brazilian government during its initial stages as a small start-up business only 10 years ago.

1   Outline how using revenue is a way of measuring the size of a business.

    Think about the way in which how much a business sells relates to its size.

    ....

    ....

2   Explain why it is difficult to compare the size of the retail business with that of a manufacturing business.

    Here you need to analyse by making links between the way that business size is measured in different industries. Think about, for example, the number of people needed to provide the service in a retailer's compared to in a manufacturing company.

    ....

    ....

    ....

    ....

    ....

    ....

3   Explain **two** reasons why the government might support start-ups like Bright Elec S.A. Which reason do you think is the most important? Justify your answer.

    Think of two reasons why governments support start-ups and explain these in context of Bright Elec S.A. Justify your answer by providing a justified decision as to which reason is the most important.

    ....

    ....

    ....

    ....

    ....

    ....

    ....

3 Enterprise, business growth and size

Activity 3.4

> The aim of this activity is to consider the reasons why organisations grow and to investigate the problems of growth.

NORDICdesign is a Danish furniture manufacturer specialising in making high-quality furniture for the domestic market. Established in 2005 as a small family-owned business, NORDICdesign has experienced significant growth over the years and is now wanting to expand its presence in international markets. Under the leadership of Karina, who assumed the role of CEO three years ago, NORDICdesign wants to grow. One method of expansion being considered by NORDICdesign is the buying of a local furniture manufacturer in Sweden.

1 Identify **two** ways NORDICdesign could expand its business.

....

....

2 Outline **two** advantages NORDICdesign might get from growing its business.

Think about the ways the business might gain from being a larger organisation.

....

....

....

....

3 Explain **two** problems NORDICdesign might face as it expands. Which problem do you think is the most significant for NORDICdesign? Justify your answer.

Try to set out the problems to NORDICdesign growth and analyse the impact of these problems on the company.

....

....

....

....

....

....

> **TIP**
>
> The best way to approach 'explain' questions is to make links between points in the question to show your analytical skills. In this question, try to reason links between the problems that you identify and their effect on NORDICdesign.

Activity 3.5

> **This activity makes you think about issues facing small businesses.**

Carmen is planning to open her first business, a small ice cream parlour that sells organic ice cream in Spain. The ice cream she intends to serve will be made using locally sourced ingredients, which is very popular with local people. Her emphasis will be on high-quality, natural ingredients and providing excellent value for money. Carmen is skilled in making traditional ice cream and she aims to employ individuals who share her passion for creating unique and delicious flavours. However, the local ice cream market is highly competitive. When Carmen approached the bank for a loan, they told Carmen that she was in a strong position to succeed but warned her about the high risk of business failure among new small businesses. The bank also expressed concern about her lack of experience in running a business.

1. Identify **four** reasons why new business start-ups might fail.

    Remember that you just need to make a list of reasons here.

    ....

    ....

    ....

    ....

2. Outline **two** reasons why Carmen's business might be successful.

    Think about the strengths Carmen has when she starts her business.

    ....

    ....

    ....

    ....

3   Enterprise, business growth and size

3 Explain **two** challenges Carmen might face when she starts her business. Which challenge do you think is likely to be the most important to Carmen? Justify your answer.

Begin your answer by explaining the challenges Carmen faces, such as her inexperience as a business owner and the competitiveness of the market. Evaluate your answer by providing a justified decision as to which problem is likely to be the most significant to Carmen.

....

....

....

....

....

....

....

....

REFLECTION

Consider the things that you have learnt in this chapter and how you can improve your written answers. How good are you at using the case study material to support the points you make? Using examples is something you can improve on when you are answering questions.

> Chapter 4
Types of business organisations

LEARNING INTENTIONS

By the end of this chapter, you will be able to:

- identify the different types of business organisations – sole traders, partnerships, private and public limited companies
- explain the advantages and disadvantages of the different types of business organisations
- recommend the best type of business organisation to use in a given situation
- understand the different forms of business organisations – franchises, joint ventures and social enterprises
- explain the advantages and disadvantages of franchises to franchisors and franchisees
- explain the advantages and disadvantages of joint ventures.

KEY TERMS

franchise joint venture limited liability partnership

private limited company public limited company

shareholder social enterprise sole trader

Activity 4.1

This activity assesses your knowledge of different types of business organisations.

There are six businesses listed in Table 4.1. Complete the table by stating whether they are a sole tradership, partnership, a private limited company or a public limited company.

Table 4.1: The different types of business organisations

Business example	Type of business
A large supermarket chain whose shares are traded on the stock market	
Small family-owned farm shop	
A regionally based restaurant chain that has invited shareholders	
Multinational car manufacturer that is listed on the Japanese stock exchange	
Roadside car cleaning business with one owner	
Medium-sized language school with eight shareholders	

Activity 4.2

This activity assesses your understanding of the risk, ownership and liability associated with a sole tradership and a partnership.

Five years ago, Farah Awang started a taxi business providing reliable transportation services. Over time, his taxi business has flourished, earning him a reputation for delivering excellent customer service at a competitive price. He now has ten drivers working for him.

Farah aims to develop his business by offering premium chauffeur services and expanding his fleet of cars to accommodate larger events. To finance the growth in his business, he is thinking of making the business a private limited company.

1   Define 'limited liability'.

    Make sure you consider what happens when a business goes bankrupt.

    ....

    ....

2   Outline **two** differences between a private limited company and a partnership.

    Identify the features of a business's legal status and the nature of its ownership.

    ....

    ....

    ....

    ....

3 Explain **two** advantages of Farah's business becoming a private limited company.

Think about the advantages Farah's business will have in terms of finance introducing more people into the management of the firm. You need to analyse the advantages you identify by considering their implications for Farah's business.

....

....

....

....

....

....

Activity 4.3

> This activity assesses your understanding of the differences between private limited companies and public limited companies.

ABC Sports is a private limited company. It is a leading football kit manufacturer and has been producing high-quality football clothing for a decade. The company is currently under the ownership of a group of friends and family members. Recognised as a reputable local brand in Argentina, ABC Sports has experienced remarkable success in the industry.

It is now aiming to broaden its horizons and intends to expand into the international market. To enable this expansion, there is a need to acquire state-of-the-art machinery and enlarge its existing manufacturing facility. The board of directors is considering the change from a private limited company to a public limited company. However, some of the ordinary shareholders are hesitant about this transformation.

1 Identify **two** differences between a private limited company and a public limited company.

Think about the nature of shareholders when answering this question.

....

....

4 Types of business organisations

2 Outline **two** advantages ABC Sports gets from being a limited company.

Identify two benefits to a business of having a separate limited company and analyse why they might be an advantage to ABC Sports. Remember to answer the question in context.

....

....

....

....

3 Do you think the advantages to ABC of becoming a public limited company are greater than the disadvantages? Justify your answer.

Analyse the advantages and disadvantages to ABC of becoming a public limited company. Make a justified decision as to whether you think the advantages are greater than the disadvantages.

....

....

....

....

....

....

....

....

Activity 4.4

This activity assesses your understanding of franchise businesses.

Juan Gomez, a Spanish entrepreneur and sole trader, has bought a franchise called "Delicias Rápidas", a fast food franchise in Seville. Juan saw the franchise as attractive because he believed there was a demand for quick, well-made options and blended traditional Spanish flavours with modern convenience. Overcoming initial funding challenges, Juan secured funding from an investor, which gave him access to a city centre location. Juan likes the way the franchise uses quality ingredients and believes in sustainable practices.

1. Define 'sole trader'.

   Make sure that you include the number of people involved in the organisation.

   ....

   ....

2. Outline **two** characteristics of a franchise.

   Think about the nature of franchise organisations and what it means to own a franchise.

   ....

   ....

   ....

   ....

3. Explain **two** reasons why a sole trader might find it hard to compete with larger firms in the same industry.

   You need to analyse the characteristics of a sole trader.

   ....

   ....

   ....

   ....

   ....

4 Types of business organisations

4 Do you think the advantages to Juan of buying a franchise are greater than the disadvantages? Justify your answer.

Consider and explain the advantages of buying a franchise to Juan. Make a justified decision as to whether you think the advantages are greater than the disadvantages to access evaluation.

....

....

....

....

....

....

....

....

> **TIP**
>
> When comparing and choosing between two options, analyse the advantages and disadvantages of each. This will help you come to a conclusion and justify your choice.

REFLECTION

What do you need to consider when applying your knowledge to a business scenario? How well have you developed your understanding of different types of business organisations? Have the questions you have answered helped improve your understanding? Think about the answers you have written and how you can improve the way you analyse and evaluate the points you make in relation to different types of business organisations.

> Chapter 5
Business objectives and stakeholder objectives

LEARNING INTENTIONS

By the end of this chapter, you will be able to:

- identify the different objectives a business can have
- understand why objectives are important for a business
- identify different stakeholder groups and their objectives
- explain the role of different stakeholder groups in a business
- understand how the objectives of different stakeholder groups can conflict.

KEY TERMS

objective	stakeholder

Activity 5.1

This activity assesses your understanding of the nature of and reasons for business objectives.

Sahir, Rahen and Avi have had a successful three-year partnership in producing online computer games. In response to the growing demand for online computer games, they have decided to form a private limited company called RGaming.

To establish the company as a prominent player in the online gaming market, Sahir, Rahen and Avi are in the process of setting clear business objectives. These objectives will include key areas such as game design innovation, market penetration, user engagement and technological advancements within the online gaming industry.

1   State **two** types of business objectives.

   ....

   ....

2 Outline **two** objectives of RGaming as a private limited company.

Think about the objectives of businesses in terms of selling their products.

....

....

....

....

3 Explain **two** benefits RGaming would get from setting effective business objectives.

Explain how business objectives can help RGaming and analyse the implications of the two benefits you have identified.

....

....

....

....

....

....

Activity 5.2

> This activity assesses your understanding of the objectives of a social enterprise.

Supermarts Co is a private limited company. It is a well-established supermarket chain in Cambodia, with a reputation for providing a wide range of products at affordable prices. Despite its success, the company faced challenges. There has been a noticeable fall in its profits over the last two years and its cash flow has deteriorated. Increased competition from international retailers and ecommerce has put pressure on this local supermarket chain. There are concerns amongst the local community and Supermarts Co's employees that some of its stores might close.

1   Identify **two** stakeholders in Supermarts Co.

    You just need a list here.

    ....

    ....

2   Outline **two** objectives of the local community and employees as stakeholders in Supermarts Co.

    Think about the concerns of employees and the local community.

    ....

    ....

    ....

    ....

3   Explain **two** reasons why it is important for Supermarts Co to have objectives. Which reason is the most important? Justify your answer.

    Think about the reasons why having objectives is important to Supermarts Co. Evaluate by providing a justified decision as to which reason is the most important.

    ....

    ....

    ....

    ....

    ....

    ....

    ....

5 Business objectives and stakeholder objectives

Activity 5.3

This activity assesses your understanding of the different types of stakeholders and how their objectives differ.

ZED Beverages is a private limited company. It is a family-owned business specialising in premium soft drinks, operates with a manufacturing facility in Zambia and sources its main ingredients from other countries. The company has a well-trained and motivated workforce and maintains positive relationships with its suppliers. While ZED Beverages has prioritised survival over the past two years, it is now planning to expand with a focus on achieving increased profits and overall growth.

There is pressure from the local government for ZED Beverages to stop importing its ingredients from other countries and, instead, buy from suppliers in Zambia. This would benefit both the local suppliers and the Zambian economy.

1 Define 'stakeholder'.

   Make sure you give the meaning of this term clearly and accurately.

   ....

   ....

2 Outline **one** internal and **one** external stakeholder of ZED Beverages.

   Think about people who work within the organisation and the people interested in ZED Beverages who are outside the organisation.

   ....

   ....

   ....

   ....

3 Explain how the objectives of ZED Beverages might have changed as it has moved from survival to growth.

   Think about the different considerations that a business needs to think about when it starts and then once it has established itself.

   ....

   ....

   ....

   ....

> **TIP**
>
> When you are answering this 'explain' question, you need to think about different stakeholders and the different objectives they have and make the link between them.

4 Do you think ZED Beverages should change from sourcing ingredients from other countries to sourcing ingredients locally? Justify your answer.

....

....

....

....

....

....

....

....

REFLECTION

Do you think your understanding of business objectives has improved as a result of answering the questions in this chapter? How do you think you can improve your understanding? It might be good to discuss this chapter with someone else in your class to help your learning in this area.

Section 1 Practice questions

Practice question 1

ArtFlix is a private limited company that operates in the tertiary sector. It is a cinema that shows a wide range of films and offers film programs for patients and employees of a local hospital. It took over another cinema in City X two years ago. When ArtFlix started five years ago, its objective was survival. The Managing Director is currently reviewing its business objectives.

a   Define 'tertiary sector'. [2]

b   Outline **two** possible objectives for ArtFlix (other than survival). [4]

c   Explain **two** advantages to ArtFlix of operating as a private limited company. [6]

d   Explain **two** advantages to ArtFlix of taking over another business. Which advantage is likely to be the most important to ArtFlix? Justify your answer. [8]

Total available marks: 20

WORKED EXAMPLE

Question 1c

Advantage 1: Can raise finance by selling shares [K]. This can lead to more funds being available to grow the business [An] that operates in the tertiary sector [Ap].

Advantage 2: Can control who buys shares [K]. This can reduce the risk of a takeover [An] for the cinema [Ap].

Improve this answer

This is a sample answer to Practice question 1d. The answer contains some weaknesses. Read through this answer and consider how it could be improved.

Advantage 1: Taking over another business results in less competition in the market [K]. This can lead to an increase in market share [An].

Advantage 2: ArtFlix can also gain the skills and ideas of the other business [K]. These ideas could lead to a competitive advantage [An].

Justification: I think that the biggest advantage is that there is less competition which could lead to more customers. The ideas from the other business may conflict with business objectives, which could delay decision making and lead to customers going to competitors instead [E].

Your challenge

See whether you can improve this answer. The answer has not been applied to ArtFlix. Although it has qualities in terms of identifying and analysing the advantages to a business of taking over another business, there is no reference to ArtFlix specifically. There must be links back to the case study in the answer.

CASE STUDY 1

Harmonic Audio is a private limited company that operates in a competitive market. It produces high-quality headphones and is a successful business. It has high demand, good management skills and finance available to be used for day-to-day costs. Harmonic Audio adds value to its headphones in many different ways. The headphones are sold in Country X.

Li Wei started the business five years ago. She has demonstrated many characteristics of a successful entrepreneur such as innovation, determination and leadership. Li Wei regularly reviews the business plan of Harmonic Audio. She knows the importance of different elements of the business plan such as objectives, market research and finance. Harmonic Audio currently has 500 employees. Li Wei uses a democratic leadership style. She takes employees ideas into consideration before making a decision. Harmonic Audio's employees are demotivated as they have to work long hours to meet customer demand.

Harmonic Audio has grown since it started. It has experienced benefits such as economies of scale, spreading risk and increased market share. One of Li Wei's objectives is to grow Harmonic Audio over the next three years by entering new markets. One option for this is to enter Country Y by forming a joint venture with another business. This joint venture would develop a new type of headphones. Li Wei is looking at the types of government support that are available in Country Y. Many stakeholder groups are interested in the activities of the business.

Section 1 Practice questions

Appendix 1

Information about Harmonic Audio

- The business is growing very quickly.
- The business has a large marketing department and regularly develops new products.

1 a Explain **two** ways Harmonic Audio could add value to its products.

Way 1:

Explanation:

Way 2:

Explanation: [8]

b Explain how Lei Wi has demonstrated the follow characteristics of a successful entrepreneur.

Which characteristic do you think is most important? Justify your answer.

Innovation:

Determination:

Strong leadership qualities:

Conclusion: [12]

2 a Explain **two** reasons why the government in Country Y might support Harmonic Audio.

Reason 1:

Explanation:

Reason 2:

Explanation: [8]

b Consider the following **three** advantages Harmonic Audio might gain from increasing its business size:

- economies of scale
- spreading risk
- increase in market share

Which advantage do you think is the most important to Harmonic Audio? Justify your answer.

Economies of scale:

Spreading risk:

Increase in market share:

Conclusion: [12]

3 a Explain **one** advantage and **one** disadvantage to Harmonic Audio of entering Country Y by forming a joint venture.

Advantage:

Explanation:

Disadvantage:

Explanation: [8]

b Consider how each of the following factors have contributed to Harmonic Audio being a successful business. Which factor do you think is the most important?

High demand:

Good management skills:

Finance available:

Conclusion: [12]

4 a Explain why **four** stakeholders might be interested in Harmonic Audio's business activities.

Stakeholder 1:

Explanation:

Stakeholder 2:

Explanation:

Stakeholder 3:

Explanation:

Stakeholder 4:

Explanation: [8]

b Consider the importance of each of the following sections of Harmonic Audio's business plan. Which section is likely to be the most important? Justify your answer.

Objectives:

Market research:

Finance:

Conclusion: [12]

Total available marks: 80

WORKED EXAMPLE

Question 2a

Reason 1: It will increase competition in Country Y [**K**].

Explanation: This can lead to more choice for customers [**An**] as there are more businesses in the market. This is likely to lead to lower prices being charged [**An**]. Harmonic Audio are likely to be able to offer lower prices due to benefitting from economies of scale [**Ap**].

Reason 2: It will create jobs [**K**].

Explanation: This will lead to a decrease in the level of unemployment [**An**], which could increase spending in the economy [**An**] for headphones and other products [**Ap**].

Improve this answer

This is a sample answer to Case study question 3b. Read through this answer and consider how it could be improved.

Economies of scale: As Harmonic Audio grows in size, it will increase its scale of output. This will reduce the average cost.

Spreading risk: As Harmonic Audio enters a new market, this means that they can spread their risks. This increases the chance of business survival.

Increase in market share: As Harmonic Audio enters a new market, they now have a new group of customers to target.

Conclusion: I think that the biggest benefit is economies of scale. The ability to charge a lower price is likely to attract customers to buy the products, which is particularly important in a competitive market. There is no guarantee that suppliers will be negotiate a lower cost.

Your challenge

See whether you can improve this answer.

Economies of scale: There is a valid point made here about economies of scale. However, there is no development of this into a chain of analysis. Try to develop this to explain what impact this could have. It would also be beneficial to add context to the answer.

Spreading risk: Again, there is a good point made about the benefits of spreading risk, but once again there is no development. Try to add this to the answer.

Increase in market share: This is a valid and correct statement but has not been written in a way which explains the advantage to Harmonic Audio.

Conclusion: The conclusion is good as it explains why economies of scale is the most important, and also explains why increase in market share might not be. There is also context to the conclusion that makes it specific to Harmonic Audio.

Section 2
People in business

Chapter 6
Human resource management

LEARNING INTENTIONS

By the end of this chapter, you will be able to:

- describe the stages of the recruitment process and methods of selecting employees
- explain the advantages and disadvantages of internal and external recruitment
- recommend who to employ in a given situation
- explain employment contracts and the various legal controls over employment
- understand the importance of training
- explain the different types of training, and the advantages and disadvantages of each type.

KEY TERMS

curriculum vitae (CV)	external recruitment	induction training
internal recruitment	job description	off-the-job training
on-the-job training	person specification	reference

Activity 6.1

This activity aims to check your knowledge and understanding of recruitment.

Securing top-tier talent has consistently been a primary objective for Tranquil Furnishings, a leading furniture manufacturer based in Ecuador. Specialising in making high-quality furniture, the company prioritises the recruitment of well-qualified and highly skilled individuals to its workforce. Tranquil Furnishings acknowledges the importance of attracting and retaining top talent by offering competitive salaries (or pay) well above industry standards and providing generous employee benefits.

Internal recruitment is always preferred reflecting Tranquil Furnishings' commitment to recognising and nurturing existing talent. However, if a suitable candidate is not found internally, the company will use external recruitment methods to identify the right individual for the role.

6 Human resource management

1 Define 'internal recruitment'.

Be precise on your terminology with this 'define' question.

....

....

2 Explain **one** disadvantage to Tranquil Furnishings of using external recruitment.

Think about issues of hiring employees who will be new to Tranquil Furnishings.

....

....

....

....

3 Explain **two** advantages to Tranquil Furnishings of using internal recruitment. Which advantage do you think is likely to be the most important to Tranquil Furnishings? Justify your answer.

Explain two advantages of internal recruitment to Tranquil Furnishings. Evaluate by providing a justified decision as to which advantage is likely to be the most important to Tranquil Furnishings.

> **TIP**
>
> Try to think about the different factors that might influence a business when it is recruiting someone for a position in an organisation.

....

....

....

....

....

....

....

Activity 6.2

> This activity will help you to apply your knowledge of the recruitment process.

Table 6.1 sets out nine stages in the recruitment process. You need to put the stages into order from 1 to 9, 1 being the start of the process.

Table 6.1: The different stages of the recruitment process

Stage	Number order
A shortlist is selected from all the applicants.	
Application forms and job details are sent out.	
A person specification is produced.	
The business identifies the need for a new employee and carries out a job analysis.	
The right candidate is selected.	
A job description is produced.	
The job is advertised.	
Completed applications are received.	
Shortlisted candidates are interviewed.	

Activity 6.3

> This activity gets you to think about the strengths and weaknesses of on-the-job training.

Phonetic is a mobile repair shop chain aiming to improve the efficiency of its staff across different aspects of their responsibilities. This means looking at Phonetic's employees' inventory management, store presentation, device repairs and customer service. The HR Director recognises the importance of training in increasing labour productivity, with a specific emphasis on on-the-job training within their phone repair stores.

1 Define 'on-the-job training'.

　..

　..

2 Outline **two** ways Phonetic could measure its labour productivity.

　Think about the way the business can quantify the work of its employees.

　..

　..

3 Explain **two** advantages to Phonetic of using on-the-job training. Which advantage is likely to be the most important to Phonetic? Justify your answer.

Explain the advantages of on-the-job training to Phonetic. Evaluate by making a justified decision as to which advantage is the most important to Phonetic.

....

....

....

....

....

....

....

....

....

Activity 6.4

> This activity gets you to think about the impact that contract law and employment regulation have on organisations.

Plombex Polska, a plumbing supplies company based in Poland, is facing a decline in sales because of online competition entering the market. To improve competitiveness, the company has decided to introduce new technology in all its branches. There are some concerns amongst its workers about changes in their employment contracts and working conditions because of the new technology. The company also faces the burden of increased costs because of a rise in the cost of materials and an increase in the minimum wage.

1 Identify **two** details that might appear in a contract of employment.

....

....

2 Outline **two** ways the new technology introduced by Plombex Polska might be of concern to the workers.

....

....

3 Explain how an increase in the costs of materials and minimum wage might have an impact on Plombex Polska profits.

Think about the way these factors affect Plombex Polska's costs.

4 Do you think Plombex Polska should introduce new technology into its branches? Justify your answer.

Consider the advantages and disadvantages to Plombex Polska of introducing new technology. Evaluate by providing a justified decision as to whether it should introduce new technology or not.

6 Human resource management

Activity 6.5

> This activity will help you to understand the recruitment and training process.

Adventure Expeditions is a leading provider of school trips for school students that provides outdoor adventures and hands-on learning experiences. Their excursions include a range of activities, from sailing and rock climbing to trekking and exploration. Adventure Expeditions understands the importance of highly skilled staff who are not only proficient in organising enriching trips but also good at promoting the business. The company prioritises training programs and recruitment to ensure their team delivers the very best educational trip experiences. The economy is growing strongly at the moment and Adventure Expeditions needs to recruit new staff.

1 Define 'job description'.

   ....

   ....

2 Identify **four** stages in the recruitment process for Adventure Expeditions employees.

   ....

   ....

   ....

   ....

> **TIP**
>
> For 'identify' questions, you just need to write a list of the specific terms.

3 Outline how Adventure Expeditions might use off-the-job training with its employees.

   Give an example of off-the-job training, such as training at a local college.

   ....

   ....

   ....

   ....

4 Explain **two** advantages to Adventure Expeditions of using off-the-job training.

Remember to make the link between the type of off-the-job training and how Adventure Expeditions might benefit, such as employees being able to focus on their training rather than their day-to-day work.

....

....

....

....

....

....

5 Explain **two** reasons why Adventure Expeditions might find it difficult to recruit new employees in an economy experiencing high levels of GDP growth. Which reason is likely to be the most important to Adventure Expeditions? Justify your answer.

Think about the issues Adventure Expeditions would face if many firms are trying to recruit staff when the economy is growing.

....

....

....

....

....

....

....

REFLECTION

Consider what you have learnt about the recruitment, selection and training of employees. Are you more confident in applying your skills to questions about recruitment and training? What would you like to continue to work on?

Chapter 7
Organisation and management

LEARNING INTENTIONS

By the end of this chapter, you will be able to:

- understand the main functional areas of a business
- interpret simple organisation charts
- understand the different methods of working, including the difference between full-time and part-time employees
- describe the functions of management
- understand the importance of delegation
- explain the advantages and disadvantages of the main leadership styles
- recommend a suitable leadership style in a given situation
- understand why reducing the size of the workforce is necessary
- recommend which workers should be made redundant in a given situation
- describe what a trade union is
- explain the benefits to employees of being members of a trade union.

KEY TERMS

autocratic leadership   chain of command   delegation
democratic leadership   flexible hours   flexible working   hierarchy
home-working   laissez-faire leadership   organisational structure
redundancy   span of control   trade union

Activity 7.1

This activity checks your knowledge and understanding of how different types of workers fit into a business's hierarchy when it is organised by function.

Table 7.1 sets out different jobs in an organisation. Complete the table by stating which functional area the job is in. The activities are:

- finance
- marketing
- operations
- human resources.

TIP

'State' questions ask you to express your answer simply and in clear terms.

Table 7.1: The different functional areas employees can work in

Job type	Functional area
Production engineer	
Accounts assistant	
Staff who hire new workers	
Social media manager	

Activity 7.2

> This activity aims to get you to focus on the span of control and the factors that affect it.

Dembe oversees a medium-sized family-owned chain of nail bars, Hot Nails, situated in a bustling city in Uganda and its nearby areas. Over the years, as the business has expanded, the hierarchy has increase number of layers. The newly appointed CEO, Karabo, is determined to streamline the organisational structure by reducing these layers. This change will impact managers as they will experience an expansion in their span of control under Dembe's leadership.

1   Define 'span of control'.

   Set out what is meant by this term in a clear and precise way.

   ....

   ....

2   Explain how the expansion of Hot Nails might have affected the span of control of its managers.

   Consider how an increasing number of workers affects the way Hot Nails is managed.

   ....

   ....

   ....

   ....

3 Explain **two** disadvantages to Hot Nails of the increase in the span of control. Which disadvantage is likely to be the most important to Hot Nails? Justify your answer.

Consider the link between the number of subordinates responsible to a manager and how this might make it more difficult for Hot Nails managers, and evaluate which disadvantage is likely to be the most significant to Hot Nails.

....

....

....

....

....

....

....

....

Activity 7.3

This activity is about the way that leadership styles affect an organisation.

Beatflow Tunes is a music streaming business led by Syed and Kazi, siblings with distinct roles – Syed as the CEO and Kazi as the financial director. Their management styles are very different. Syed wants to have control over decision-making, making all major choices and rarely delegating tasks. On the other hand, Kazi wants to involve others in decision-making approach.

Recognising the weakness in their leadership styles, an investor has urged Beatflow Tunes to change to a more democratic approach.

1 Outline **two** characteristics of the autocratic leadership style of management.

Try to give examples of how autocratic managers manage their subordinates and take decisions.

....

....

....

....

2 Explain **two** advantages to Beatflow of using a democratic leadership style. Which advantage is likely to be the most significant to Beatflow? Justify your answer.

Explain two advantages to Beatflow of using a democratic leadership style. Evaluate by providing a justified decision as to which advantage is likely to be the most important to Beatflow.

....

....

....

....

....

....

....

....

Activity 7.4

> **In this activity, you need to show your knowledge of the different functions of management.**

The following are the functions of management:

- planning
- organising
- commanding
- coordinating
- controlling.

7 Organisation and management

Match the examples of the work of managers with each of the functions in Table 7.2.

Make sure that you are clear on the meanings of the individual words used to describe managerial functions as it will help you understand what each type of manager does.

Table 7.2: Examples of the different functions of management

Example	Function
The sales figures of individual sales managers are reported to the sales director.	
A production manager holds regular meetings with their subordinates to make sure they are achieving the right quality of products.	
Directors have a meeting to decide on a marketing strategy for a new product.	
The marketing director puts together material for the marketing team to be used in a presentation.	
A human resources manager works with a sales manager to decide on the recruitment of a new salesperson.	

Activity 7.5

> This activity encourages you to show your knowledge and understanding of democratic management along with the relationship between management and trade unions.

The leadership team at Fast Print Solutions is dealing with challenging industrial relations issues between the company's management and its workforce. Numerous industrial disputes have resulted in significant losses in terms of both labour productivity and damage to the company's reputation with its customers. In response, the directors have put together a strategy aimed at using democratic leadership and delegation. Fast Print Solutions also wants to improve relations with the trade union that represents a substantial portion of the company's workforce.

1 Define 'delegation'.

Be precise in the way set out what this term means.

....

....

2 Outline **two** roles of the trade union operating at Fast Print Solutions.

Think about the ways the trade union at Fast Print Solutions might represent their members.

....

....

....

....

3 Explain **two** reasons Fast Print Solutions might benefit from democratic leadership.

Consider how the increased involvement of the workforce in decision-making might be an advantage for Fast Print Solutions.

....

....

....

....

....

....

> **TIP**
>
> Be analytical with 'explain' questions by making links between the advantages of democratic leadership and how this might affect Fast Print Solutions.

4 Do you think the advantages to Fast Print Solutions employees of being trade union members are greater than the disadvantages? Justify your answer.

Start this answer by explaining the advantages to Fast Print Solutions's employees of being trade union members. Then consider what the disadvantages might be. Evaluate by providing a justified decision as to whether the advantages are greater than the disadvantages.

....

....

....

....

7 Organisation and management

....

....

....

....

Activity 7.6

> This activity checks your knowledge and understanding of when businesses downsize and how this leads to redundancies.

Lusitano Cutlery is an established Portuguese cutlery manufacturing company that has recently announced significant downsizing due to financial difficulties. Lusitano Cutlery is known as a high-quality cutlery brand. However, increased competition from lower cost overseas producers has adversely affected its profitability and cash flow position.

The directors of Lusitano Cutlery have responded to its challenging financial position by downsizing the business and making 25% of the workforce redundant. The directors see this as the best way of ensuring the long-term security of the company.

Lusitano Cutlery's CEO, Maria Silva, has put together a plan of how the downsizing of the business can be done most effectively, which includes redundancy along with redundancy payments.

1 Define 'downsizing'.

....

....

2 Outline **two** factors a business might consider when deciding who to make redundant.

....

....

....

....

BUSINESS FOR CAMBRIDGE IGCSE™ AND O LEVEL: WORKBOOK

3 Explain how increased foreign competition could have affected Lusitano Cutlery's cash flow and profitability.

....

....

....

....

....

4 Do you think the advantages to Lusitano Cutlery of downsizing its business are greater than the disadvantages? Justify your answer.

....

....

....

....

....

....

REFLECTION

Consider what you have learnt about the way that different organisations are organised and managed. How effectively have you used the work of the different management theorists in your answers to the questions? Check your answers to see whether you are using management theorists in your writing.

Chapter 8
Methods of communication

LEARNING INTENTIONS

By the end of this chapter, you will be able to:

- understand why communication is important for a business
- identify different communication methods, both internal and external
- explain the advantages and disadvantages of different methods of communication
- recommend and justify a suitable method of communication to use in a given situation
- identify examples of communication barriers
- understand the reasons for and problems caused by communication barriers
- explain how communication barriers can be reduced or removed.

KEY TERM

communication barrier

Activity 8.1

This activity will help you check your knowledge of internal and external communication.

Table 8.1 sets out the types of communication used by an Indian supermarket chain called Krishna's Superstore. Complete the table by identifying whether the method of communication is internal or external.

Table 8.1: Different methods of communication Krishna's Superstore can use

Example	Internal/external
An email is sent by senior managers to Krishna's Superstore employees about health and safety at work.	
Krishna's Superstore conducts an online survey with potential customers.	
Krishna's Superstore CEO has a face-to-face meeting with an investor.	
The Finance Director of Krishna's Superstore has a weekly online meeting with their finance team.	

(Continued)

Table 8.1: (Continued)

Example	Internal/external
Krishna's Superstore has a town hall meeting with local residents who live near one of its stores.	
A monthly newsletter is sent by email to all the store managers in Krishna's Superstore.	

Activity 8.2

This activity gets you to think about effective communication.

Alk Architects is a medium-sized architectural firm based in South Africa. The firm's CEO, Alex, views effective communication as fundamental to the success of the business. He emphasises, 'As a firm centred around design and collaboration, it's important that we communicate effectively with all our stakeholders.' Alex places significant importance on face-to-face communication within the organisation and wants employees to 'engage in direct discussions whenever possible, especially if they are in the same building.' By using this two-way communication Alex believes communication barriers can be broken down.

1   Define 'communication barrier'.

   Remember to be clear and precise when you are defining this term.

   ....

   ....

2   Outline how two-way communication takes place in Alk Architects.

   Consider how information passes back and forth between groups and individuals in Alk Architects.

   ....

   ....

3   Identify **four** types of communication methods.

   You just need a list of types of communication methods here.

   ....

   ....

   ....

   ....

8 Methods of communication

4 Explain **two** ways effective communication might be useful to Alk Architects.

   Consider the importance of feedback as an advantage of effective communication.

   ....

   ....

   ....

   ....

   ....

   ....

> **TIP**
>
> In the 'explain' question of this case study, make the link between effective communication and how it might be an advantage to Alk Architects. By making effective links, you will develop your evaluative skills when you are answering questions.

5 Do you think the management at Alk Architects should encourage greater use of face-to-face communication in their organisation? Justify your answer.

   Consider the advantages and disadvantages to Alk Architects of using face-to-face communication.

   ....

   ....

   ....

   ....

   ....

   ....

   ....

   ....

   ....

Activity 8.3

> **In this activity, you need to think about the strengths and weaknesses of two types of communication methods.**

QuickRail operates a network of railway services across the country. The management team at QuickRail employs various communication channels to interact with their employees. To streamline communication, QuickRail has introduced a dedicated mobile application that provides regular text message updates and information to all staff members. Additionally, email serves as a primary method of communication for important announcements and correspondence. Despite these efforts, some employees have expressed concern regarding the volume of messages from QuickRail.

1   Identify **four** types of communication.

    ....

    ....

    ....

    ....

2   Explain why email serves as a primary method of communication for important announcements at QuickRail.

    Think about the speed and coverage of email communication.

    ....

    ....

    ....

    ....

3   Explain **two** reasons why employees at QuickRail are concerned about the volume of text messages and emails from Quickrail. Which reason is likely to be the most important to QuickRail? Justify your answer.

Explain the problems by considering the link between a high number of text messages and emails and their productivity.

....

....

....

....

....

....

....

Activity 8.4

This activity aims to make you look at the problems and solutions to poor communication.

HopCar, a car rental company based in Australia, is facing significant operational challenges stemming from ineffective communication across its organisation. A recent report produced by a management consultancy firm on the company's communication methods shows considerable problems related to Hopcar's choice of communication channels, inadequate two-way communication and long communication channels. The management consultant has recommended that HopCar use more face-to-face meetings to improve its communication.

1   Identify **four** types of communication barrier.

....

....

....

....

2 Explain **one** reason why technical barriers and **one** reason why cultural barriers might lead to poor communication at HopCar.

Consider the way that communication barriers work and how they can affect communication at HopCar.

....

....

....

....

3 Explain how poor communication might affect HopCar's costs and employee motivation.

Think about the implications of poor communication for decision-making at HopCar.

....

....

....

....

....

....

4 Do you think the advantages to HopCar of using face-to-face communication are greater than the disadvantages? Justify your answer.

Consider the advantages and disadvantages to HopCar of using face-to-face communication.

....

....

....

....

....

....

....

> **TIP**
>
> Make sure that you use the case study organisation as much as you can to illustrate your answer to the questions. This will show how you understand the context of the points you are making and how the points you make in an answer relate to a business.

Activity 8.5

This activity helps you to practise answering questions on the different aspects of communication within organisations.

A charitable organisation based in Tunisia called Y2J Charity has very strong ties to the local community and is looking to improve communication across its operations. Y2J Charity uses traditional communication methods such as written letters and noticeboards. However, the management is troubled by the absence of effective two-way communication and feedback mechanisms. Given Y2J Charity's modest size, managers regularly engage in verbal communication with their team members. To address these communication challenges, the management wants to implement an intranet and mobile device system to improve communication and information sharing within the organisation.

1 How might managers in Y2J Charity receive feedback from its employees?

Think about the nature of feedback in an organisation.

....

....

2 Explain **two** reasons why the use of email might lead to inefficient communication at Y2J Charity.

Look at the way emails are used in organisations and the problems that might arise from this.

....

....

....

....

....

....

3 Do you think the advantages to Y2J of using electronic communication are greater than the disadvantages? Justify your answer.

Explain the advantages and disadvantages to Y2J of using text messages and emails and decide whether the advantages are greater than the disadvantages.

....

....

....

....

....

....

....

....

REFLECTION

Do you feel that you are getting better at responding to the different types of questions you answering with each case study? Is this reflected in the marks you are getting from your teacher? You could improve on this by discussing your use of case study material with someone else in your class.

> Chapter 9
Motivating employees

> **LEARNING INTENTIONS**
>
> By the end of this chapter, you will be able to:
> - identify the reasons why people work
> - explain the importance of motivation in the workplace
> - understand the three main theories of motivation
> - explain financial and non-financial methods of motivation
> - recommend a suitable method of motivation for a business to use in a given situation.

> **KEY TERMS**
>
> bonus   commission   employee of the month
> fringe benefits   hygiene factors   job enrichment   job rotation
> labour turnover   motivators   piece-rate
> profit sharing   salary   time-based

Activity 9.1

> This activity provides a chance to demonstrate your knowledge of why people work.

Table 9.1 sets out some quotes from employees at ARC Cleaning, a medium-sized private limited company based in Ecuador, relating to factors that affected them in their work. Match the factors listed with the quotes given:

- pay
- fringe benefits
- promotion
- training
- status
- responsibility
- interesting work
- friendship.

Table 9.1: Factors that motivate employees at work

Quote	Reason
'I enjoy talking to my colleagues at lunch.'	
'I like leading on a project and managing it right through to the end.'	
'I like being offered free health insurance for working at the company.'	
'I like the fact the company pays more than its competitors.'	
'I like the opportunities for promotion at the business.'	
'I really enjoy the complex problems we have to work on because they are so interesting.'	
'I like the way the business rewards workers with an employee of the month award.'	
'I like the way the company offers all the staff the opportunity to go on courses.'	

Activity 9.2

> This activity aims to look at the link between employee motivation and productivity, absenteeism and labour turnover.

ELM is a prominent public limited company that manufactures computer components with its production facilities distributed globally. Among its factories, one stands out as a top performer in terms of labour productivity, absenteeism and labour turnover within the computer component manufacturing sector. Sergey, the CEO of the factory, thinks the business's success to the highly effective management of its workforce.

1   Outline what absenteeism and labour turnover indicate.

   Remember to set out how these two factors affect the workforce.

   ....

   ....

   ....

   ....

> **TIP**
>
> 'Outline' questions want you to set out the main points the question is asking for. Here, the main points of absenteeism and labour turnover need to be set out.

9 Motivating employees

2 Explain how ELM would measure labour productivity.

Explain how ELM can measure its output relative to input.

....

....

....

....

3 Explain why well-motivated employees might have lower levels of absenteeism and labour turnover.

Make the link between how satisfied employees are at work and how often they are absent from work or leave their jobs.

....

....

....

....

4 Do you think effective management is the best way to increase ELM's labour productivity? Justify your answer.

....

....

....

....

....

....

....

> **TIP**
>
> Explain the link between management and labour productivity. Try to analyse how good management can increase productivity. Evaluate your argument by considering other factors that might increase productivity.

Activity 9.3

> This activity gets you to look at the application of Maslow's hierarchy of needs.

RCG Drugs is a local chain of regional pharmicies facing motivational challenges among its staff. Table 9.2 outlines statements from its employees. Align each quote from the table with the various levels in Maslow's hierarchy of needs to analyse the motivational factors within the organisation:

- physiological
- safety
- social
- esteem
- self-actualisation.

Table 9.2: Statements from RCG Drugs employees and the related level in Maslow's hierarchy of needs

Quote	Need
'I feel a bit isolated in the work I do and I spend too much time on my own.'	
'I do not have enough time to eat my lunch so am hungry in the afternoon.'	
'Some of the tasks I am allocated in the shop do not challenge me.'	
'I am concerned about my job security because I know the business has financial problems.'	
'I keep being passed over for promotion and I don't receive any thanks or recognition for the work I do.'	

Activity 9.4

> In this activity, you have to apply Herzberg's two-factor theory and Taylor's scientific management to an organisation.

Collar is a private limited company. It is a leading shirt manufacturing firm based in Italy and operates with a dedicated workforce of 40 employees on the production line, striving to meet specific production goals. The demanding nature of these targets places considerable pressure on the workers; however, it is worth noting that Collar offers some of the most competitive salaries in the industry. Recently, the company has welcomed a new CEO with a vision to reshape the organisational culture, changing from the principles of Taylor's 'scientific management theory' to Herzberg's 'two-factor theory'.

9 Motivating employees

1. Identify **two** features associated with the Taylor's 'scientific management theory' that Collar uses.

   With an 'identify' question you just need to list two features.

   ....

   ....

2. Outline **two** hygiene factors that Collar might use if it changes to the Herzberg's 'two-factor theory'.

   Think about and set out the main points of hygiene factors such as pay and conditions.

   ....

   ....

   ....

   ....

3. Explain **two** ways Herzberg's two-factor theory could improve the motivation of Collar's employees. Which way do you think is the most important to Collar? Justify your answer.

   Consider how hygiene factors and motivators can improve motivation at Collar.

   ....

   ....

   ....

   ....

   ....

   ....

   ....

Activity 9.5

> This activity helps you to develop your knowledge and application of financial rewards.

Table 9.3 contains a list of different types of financial rewards. Match each of these rewards to the example given.

| hourly wage rate | salary | piece-rate | commission |
| bonus scheme | fringe benefit | profit sharing | |

Table 9.3: The different types of financial reward used by business organisations

Example	Financial reward
The salespeople for a photocopying business are paid a fixed amount if they achieve their sales target.	
Exam markers are paid a set amount of money for each exam script they mark.	
Hospital doctors are paid a fixed amount of money per year for the work they do.	
Staff in a furniture shop are paid a fixed amount of money for each unit of furniture they sell.	
Staff in a fast food restaurant are given a free meal for each shift they work.	
Sales staff in a ticket office are paid £12 per hour.	
Employees receive a percentage of the business profits. The amount can depend on business (and individual) performance.	

Activity 9.6

> This activity aims to consider how non-financial methods can be used to increase motivation.

Chanlina has recently taken the role of store manager for an underperforming sports shop that is part of a retail chain. One of the primary issues she has pinpointed is a lack of motivation among the staff. To boost employee morale, Chanlina has allowed the staff to have a say in changes to the store and giving them increased responsibility in the decision-making process. She has introduced a series of alterations to working practices through incorporating job rotation and job enrichment to improve the overall performance of her team.

9 Motivating employees

1 Outline the difference between job rotation and job enrichment.

Think about and set out the key points of job rotation and job enrichment.

....

....

....

....

2 Explain **two** ways job rotation might improve the motivation of Chanlina's team.

Be analytical here by making the link between giving employees the opportunity to be involved in different activities at work and their motivation.

....

....

....

....

> **TIP**
>
> 'Explain' questions want you to give the reasons why and how they make things happen. In part b, the reason why motivation is improved need to be outlined.

3 Do you think the advantages to Chanlina of using job enrichment to improve the performance of her team are greater than the disadvantages? Justify your answer.

Explain the advantages and disadvantages to Chanlina of using job enrichment. Think about the link between job enrichment and motivation.

....

....

....

....

....

....

....

> **REFLECTION**
>
> Think about what you have learnt about what motivates people at work. Do you feel confident in analysing and evaluating the factors that motivate people at work? How do you think you could improve this? Testing yourself by discussing questions in this chapter with others in class might help you improve.

Section 2 Practice questions

Practice question 1

Smoothride Car Hire is a car rental company. It has 600 employees and 30 branches. Smoothride Car Hire's Human Resources Director is thinking about different methods to improve communication within the business. Employee motivation is low at Smoothride Car Hire. The Managing Director is thinking about changing her leadership style. She currently uses an autocratic leadership style.

a   Identify **two** methods of communication. [2]

b   Outline **two** disadvantages to Smoothride Car Hire of low employee motivation. [4]

c   Explain **two** factors that could affect the method of communication used by Smoothride Car Hire. [6]

d   Explain **two** leadership styles Smoothride Car Hire could use (other than autocratic). Which is likely to be the best style for Smoothride Car Hire to use? Justify your answer. [8]

Total available marks: 20

> **WORKED EXAMPLE**
>
> ### Question 1c
>
> Factor 1: The urgency of the message [**K**]. If the information needs to be communicated straight away, then a phone call might be the best method to use [**An**] at the car rental company [**Ap**].
>
> Factor 2: How many people need to receive the message [**K**]. If the message needs to be sent to all 600 employees [**Ap**] then a method such as emails could be used as the message can be sent to many employees at once [**An**].

Improve this answer

This is a sample answer to Practice question part d. The answer contains some weaknesses. Read through this answer and consider how it could be improved.

Leadership style 1: Democratic leadership could be used [K]. This is beneficial as employees' ideas can be taken into account [An], such as how to improve communication [Ap].

Leadership style 2: Laissez-faire could also be used [K].

Justification: I think that democratic leadership is the best method to use as taking ideas into account can lead to improved communication between managers and employees, which is currently an issue at Smoothride Car Hire.

Your challenge

See whether you can improve this answer. This answer is good for leadership style 1 as it included knowledge, application and analysis. It does not develop the knowledge point for leadership style 2 so application and analysis are missing. As the discussion is one sided, it makes it difficult to evaluate which leadership style is best to use. Once the discussion has been made more balanced, the justification can be developed to make a justified decision.

CASE STUDY 1

CleanTech manufactures cleaning products. It started up nine years ago. It is a successful business and is one of the leading businesses in the cleaning products industry in Country X. CleanTech has a 25% market share and its profits increased by 12% last year.

CleanTech has 70 highly-skilled employees. Some of its employees are full-time and some are part-time. Each employee has an employment contract that includes details such as duties and responsibilities and working hours. CleanTech pays salaries that are higher than the average for the industry. Employees at CleanTech feel valued for their contributions and enjoy developing and producing cleaning products. Its employees are highly motivated. CleanTech uses a range of methods to motivate its employees including piece-rate and opportunities for promotion.

The Managing Director is a democratic leader that involves all employees in decision-making. She also delegates tasks to some employees. CleanTech has a flat organisational structure and managers have a wide span of control. CleanTech uses electronic methods of communication to communicate with its employees. The Human Resources Director is thinking about using alternative methods of communication. She is thinking about having more meetings with employees and reducing the number of emails that are sent to employees.

CleanTech makes training its employees a priority. It uses off-the-job training. Employees are regularly sent to the local university for courses so that employees can benefit from the specialist knowledge of trainers and new ideas.

Section 2 Practice questions

1 a Explain **one** advantage and **one** disadvantage to CleanTech of using a democratic leadership style.

Advantage:

Explanation:

Disadvantage:

Explanation:

[8]

b Consider the following **three** advantages of off-the-job training. Which advantage is the most important to CleanTech? Justify your answer.

Specialised knowledge and skills of trainers:

Does not disrupt the output of other employees:

Opportunity to get new ideas:

Conclusion:

[12]

2 a Explain **one** advantage and **one** disadvantage to CleanTech of using emails to communicate with its employees.

Advantage:

Explanation:

Disadvantage:

Explanation:

[8]

b Consider the advantages and disadvantages to CleanTech of using the following **two** methods to motivate its employees: Which method do you think is most likely to motivate employees at CleanTech? Justify your answer.

Piece-rate:

Opportunities for promotion:

Conclusion:

[12]

3 a Explain **two** advantages to CleanTech of delegating some tasks to its employees.

Advantage 1:

Explanation:

Advantage 2:

Explanation:

[8]

b Consider the advantages and disadvantages to CleanTech of having full-time and part-time employees. Which type of employee is likely to be most beneficial to CleanTech?

Full-time employees:

Part-time employees:

Conclusion:

[12]

4 a Explain **two** disadvantages to CleanTech of its managers having a wide span of control.

Disadvantage 1:

Explanation:

Disadvantage 2:

Explanation:

[8]

b Consider the reasons why the following **two** elements of an employment contract are important to CleanTech. Which element is likely to be the most important? Justify your answer.

Duties and responsibilities:

Working hours:

Conclusion:

[12]

Total available marks: 80

WORKED EXAMPLE

Question 3b

Full-time: There is a consistent standard of work produced [K], which can lead to an increase in the reputation of the business. This can lead to an increase in sales and revenue [An] when selling cleaning products [Ap]. However, there are fewer employees available to cover if someone is absent [K], which can decrease output levels of the business and make it harder to meet customer demand [An].

Part-time: Do not need to pay wages when employees are not working [K]. This can lower the variable costs of CleanTech, which can reduce the break-even point [An]. However, there may be a lower quality of service if customers have to wait longer for a part-time employee to deal with their request [K]. This could decrease brand image [An].

Conclusion: I think that full-time employees are more likely to be the most important as consistency of service can increase customer loyalty which can increase market share from 25% [Ap]. Part-time employees may be more difficult to communicate with which could increase mistakes and increase costs, eliminating the benefit of the cost saving from a lower wage bill [E].

Improve this answer

Here is a sample answer to Case study question 2a. Read through this answer and consider how it could be improved.

Advantage 1: Emails can be referred back to [K].

Explanation: This means the 70 employees [Ap] can look back at the message if they need to.

Disadvantage 2: The message may go into junk mail [K].

Explanation: If messages go into junk mail then employees may not see them. This could lead to tasks not being completed [An].

Your challenge

See whether you can improve this answer. This answer has some good features. Advantage 1 is a relevant knowledge point and has made clear reference to the case study. However, this point has not been developed into a chain of analysis – two points of development are required.

Advantage 2 is also a relevant knowledge point and there is some development of this into analysis. Further analysis is needed, as well as application to the case study.

Section 3
Marketing

Chapter 10
Marketing and the market

LEARNING INTENTIONS

By the end of this chapter, you will be able to:

- outline the role of marketing
- identify why markets change and how businesses respond
- calculate market share
- understand the difference between niche markets and mass markets
- explain how markets can be segmented and the advantages and disadvantages of doing so.

KEY TERMS

market segmentation   market share   marketing

mass market   niche market

Activity 10.1

This activity helps you understand how the market affects business.

Meteor Newspapers is a prominent news publication based in California, USA. The business has set its sights on expanding its customer base to appeal to the mass market and establishing its position as a leading source of news and information in the region. The business faces the challenge of a rapidly changing digital media landscape and changing consumer preferences when it comes to consuming news. The business was established in 1998 and has been recognised for its commitment to journalistic standards and its comprehensive coverage of local, national and global events. In recent years, the newspaper industry has faced the challenges of declining print readership and increased competition from digital media platforms. In response to this, Meteor has used extensive market research to guide its developing digital presence. The business now focuses on online news rather than printed newspapers.

TIP

When you are answering marketing questions, think about the buying behaviour of consumers and how a business's decisions affect their buying behaviour.

10 Marketing and the market

1 Define 'mass market'.

Make sure you use precise terminology here.

....

....

2 Outline **two** ways the news media market has changed in recent years.

Think about the way technology has affected the news media market.

....

....

....

....

3 Explain **two** ways Meteor could use market research to find out about consumers in the news media market.

Think about the methods businesses use to find out about the behaviour of their customers.

....

....

....

....

....

Activity 10.2

> This activity provides an opportunity for you to practise applying your knowledge of factors affecting consumer demand.

In Table 10.1, match the reason why the sales of a product might change and the examples given from different markets.

Table 10.1: The reason why the sales of a product might change, with examples

Reason	Example
The price of the product	The demand for new cars increases after average wages in the economy increase.
The price of competitors' products	The revenues of a soft drinks manufacturer decrease because the price of the soft drinks of another manufacturer has decreased.
Changes in consumer income	An online promotion campaign increases the sales of a business that sells electric heaters.
Changes in tastes and fashion	A retailer that sells reading glasses has experienced a rise in revenues over the last ten years because an ageing population is more likely to need reading glasses.
Spending on advertising and promotion	A budget airline experiences a rise in demand for flights on holiday routes because it has introduced discounts on these routes.
Changes in population size and structure	A chain of coffee shops has seen its sales rise because more people enjoy socialising during the day.

Activity 10.3

> This activity helps to develop your understanding of the impact of the external environment on marketing.

Nordic Maps AS is a cartography (map publishing) company based in Norway. It is a business with a great history, with over a century of experience publishing and distributing maps across Norway and globally. Nordic Maps has encountered significant challenges in recent years with the development of online mapping services and the use of digital maps that has reshaped the map industry. Nordic Maps has also had to face the challenge of a rise in Norway's minimum wage and the implementation of strict health and safety regulations. An additional pressure on the business is increased international competition from overseas producers.

10 Marketing and the market

1 Identify **four** factors in the external environment that are currently affecting Nordic Maps.

   You just need to make a list of factors here.

   ....

   ....

   ....

   ....

2 Outline how an increase in the minimum wage and new health and safety regulations might increase Nordic Maps' costs.

   Try to say how regulations and wages might increase costs, such as how a rise in the minimum wage might increase Nordic Maps' labour costs. Try to use an example to support this.

   ....

   ....

   ....

   ....

Activity 10.4

In this activity, you need to think about niche markets and mass markets.

Sodafresh Nigeria is a large multinational corporation specialising in the production of soft drinks for consumers across Nigeria. Among its leading brands is the beverage line known as Freshfizz, which has a significant market share within the soft drinks market in Nigeria. Under the leadership of Aarin as CEO, Sodafresh has recently completed the purchase of a small company well known for its premium quality soft drinks, which are priced at twice the price of Sodafresh's existing products. This newly acquired brand caters to a niche market segment comprising affluent consumers, further diversifying Sodafresh's product portfolio and expanding its presence in the high-end beverage market.

1 Define 'niche market'.

   ....

   ....

2 Outline the difference between niche markets and mass markets.

Think about the way markets can be looked at in broad terms and narrow terms.

....

....

....

....

3 Explain **two** advantages to Sodafresh of operating in a mass market.

Consider the advantages of selling large quantities of goods in a market.

....

....

....

....

....

....

4 Do you think the advantages to Sodafresh operating in a niche market are greater than the disadvantages? Justify your answer.

Start your answer by considering the advantages to Sodafresh of operating in a niche market, and then consider the disadvantages. Evaluate by providing a justified decision as to whether the advantages to Sodafresh are greater than the disadvantages.

....

....

....

....

....

....

> **TIP**
>
> 'Justify' means making a reasoned argument that is supported by evidence on how moving into a different market segment might benefit Sodafresh.

....

....

Activity 10.5

In this activity, you need to consider the strengths and weaknesses of market segmentation.

Aquagear Greece is a leading swimwear manufacturer with the aim of strategic growth over the next five years. The company is looking to develop its market presence in the sports swimwear industry by focusing on three key market segments: young club swimmers, serious club swimmers and elite-level swimmers. To achieve this goal, Aquagear is developing innovative swimwear designs tailored to the needs and preferences of each segment. Additionally, the company is changing its promotional strategies to effectively reach and engage its target audience, ensuring its position as a frontrunner in the Greek sports swimwear market. Aquagear designs its products to reach the target market segments and promote its products in a way that will attract the target market segments.

1 Define 'market segment'.

....

....

2 Outline **two** ways Aquagear Greece can target young club swimmers as part of its strategic growth plan.

   Think about the types of consumers Aquagear is trying to sell to and support your answer with examples.

....

....

....

....

3 Do you think the advantages to Aquagear Greece of using market segmentation are greater than the disadvantages? Justify your answer.

Explain the advantages and disadvantages to Aquagear Greece of using market segmentation. Evaluate by providing a justified decision as to whether the advantages to Aquagear are greater than the disadvantages.

....

....

....

....

....

....

....

....

....

....

....

....

....

REFLECTION

This chapter is designed to develop your understanding of the different ways that businesses can look at their market. Consider what you have learnt about the different ways that businesses plan and react to different parts of their markets. Which areas do you most need to focus on and improve?

> Chapter 11
Market research

> **LEARNING INTENTIONS**
>
> By the end of this chapter, you will be able to:
>
> - understand and explain the role of market research
> - identify primary and secondary methods of market research and explain the advantages and disadvantages of each
> - explain the factors influencing the accuracy of market research
> - analyse simple market research data.

> **KEY TERMS**
>
> market research   primary research   sampling   secondary research

Activity 11.1

> The aim of this activity is to get you to think about how an organisation uses market research to focus on consumer needs.

Le Electric is a prominent electricity provider operating in various regions of France. Recent media coverage has highlighted significant concerns regarding the company's customer service standards. Criticisms have centred around prolonged power cuts and poor communication with customers. In response to these challenges, a new management team has been appointed to improve Le Electric's customer service and overall image.

An important part of the new management's strategy is the implementation of effective market research. The new management team sees the importance of improving the business's customer service.

1   Define 'market research'.

   Use precise terms with definition questions.

   ....

   ....

2 Outline **two** types of primary market research Le Electric could use to find out about its customer needs.

Consider the ways Le Electric can find out about the needs of its customers.

....

....

....

....

> **TIP**
>
> To 'outline', you need to describe the types of market research used by Le Electric.

3 Explain **two** reasons why Le Electric uses market research. Which reason do you think is the most important to Le Electric? Justify your answer.

Evaluate your answer by deciding upon the most important reason why market research is used by Le Electric and justifying your answer.

....

....

....

....

....

....

....

Activity 11.2

> **In this activity, you need to show your knowledge of the difference between primary research and secondary research.**

Table 11.1 sets out examples of different types of market research conducted by a chain of florists (flower shops). Complete the table by identifying whether the types of research are primary research or secondary research.

Table 11.1: Different types of market research conducted by chain of florists

Example	Type of research
The owner of the florist buys a market research report produced by a market research agency.	
A focus group is invited to the florist to discuss its products.	
A member of staff spends time each week looking at online articles related to the florist market.	
The manager of the florist sets up an online questionnaire for customers to complete when they are ordering flowers.	
The florist uses government data to find out about changes in demography and income in the areas where its shops are located.	
The sales assistants at the florists are told to ask targeted questions to customers when they are buying products.	

Activity 11.3

This activity gets you to focus on the application of primary research.

Amadis, the CEO of Choclet, a Sri Lankan confectionery manufacturer, is moving the company towards a new market position. There has been a decline in the sales of its products because of concerns over sugary snacks targeted at children. The company wants to launch a new upmarket product range targeted at adults. The product will be marketed as an exclusive chocolate bar with a high cocoa content and sold at a premium price. This strategic repositioning of Choclet's product range is based on changing consumer preferences in the confectionery market. By using this approach and based on extensive primary research and secondary data analysis, Amadis believes it can grow Choclet's market share in the premium segment of the chocolate bar market.

1 Outline the difference between primary and secondary market research.

Thinks about the two different sources of market research Choclet can use.

....

....

2 State **two** types of primary research that Choclet might have used.

   You just need to list the types of primary research with a state question.

   ....

   ....

3 Explain **two** advantages to Choclet of using secondary research to increase its understanding of the confectionery market.

   Here you need to focus on, for example, how secondary research might help get information that is precisely related to the Sri Lankan confectionery market.

   ....

   ....

   ....

   ....

   ....

   ....

> **TIP**
>
> The 'explain' activity 11.3 3 wants you to make links between factors identified in a question.

4 Explain **two** advantages to Choclet of using primary market research. Which advantage do you think is the most important to Choclet? Justify your answer.

   ....

   ....

   ....

   ....

   ....

   ....

   ....

Activity 11.4

> **In this activity, you can practise applying your skills in interpreting and analysing data from charts.**

RRL is a market research company that provides strategic insights to businesses, helping them to develop their marketing strategies. RRL has been approached by a media business to research the news media market. In response to the growing importance of online sales in the news media market, RRL conducted market research on online buying patterns among a sample group of consumers. The aim was to offer valuable insights to businesses looking to improve their online marketing strategies. RRL collected data on the online purchasing behaviour of a sample group of 50 consumers from 2022 to 2024. Each member of the sample group was tracked as to whether they bought online newspapers or print newspapers during this period.

Table 11.1: Online purchasing behaviour of 40 consumers from 2022 to 2024

Year	Buying an online newspaper	Buying a print newspaper
2022	24	26
2023	32	18
2024	41	9

1. Define 'sampling'.

   ....

   ....

2. **a** Calculate the percentage increase in the sample buying their newspaper online from 2022 to 2024.

   ....

   ....

   b Calculate the percentage of the sample buying a print newspaper in 2022 and in 2024.

   Remember to clearly show your working when you are doing a calculation question.

   ....

   ....

BUSINESS FOR CAMBRIDGE IGCSE™ AND O LEVEL: WORKBOOK

   c   Outline what has happened to the news media market from 2022 to 2024.

   Set out clearly what your calculations show about the trend in news media market.

   ....

   ....

3 Explain **two** advantages of RRL using sampling as part of its market research.

   Think about the advantages of using restricted data rather than trying to get information from the whole market.

   ....

   ....

   ....

   ....

   ....

   ....

> ### REFLECTION
>
> As you finish this chapter, reflect on your understanding of how organisations use market research to improve their marketing strategies for their products. What do you need to do to improve your understanding? Try to find an example of a business doing market research and see what you can learn from it.

Chapter 12
Marketing mix: product

LEARNING INTENTIONS

By the end of this chapter, you will be able to:

- explain the advantages and disadvantages of developing new products
- explain the importance of brand image
- explain the role of packaging
- identify the main stages of the product life cycle and understand a product life cycle diagram
- understand examples of extension strategies that a business could use, and explain their advantages and disadvantages
- recommend and justify an extension strategy to use in a given situation.

KEY TERMS

brand image   extension strategies   marketing mix   product life cycle

Activity 12.1

This activity is designed to help you check your understanding of new product development.

Carry-on is a Turkish rucksack manufacturer that manufactures premium quality backpacks. The business is successful because of its strong brand image. Its most successful product is a range of large hiking backpacks designed for outdoor enthusiasts, priced by retailers at $200–$300. The backpack market is very competitive and Carry-on is continually exploring innovative product developments and designs. In response to the launch of a new product by a major competitor, Carry-on is preparing to launch a new line of ultra-lightweight backpacks. Carry-on has invested heavily in product design, extensive market research and product testing to make the launch of the new ultra-light backpacks a success.

1   Define 'brand image'.

   Remember to use precise terminology with this define question.

   ....

   ....

2 Explain **two** reasons why Carry-on would want to introduce its new ultralight backpack.

Consider how Carry-on might have to respond to changes in the market and consumer preferences.

....

....

....

....

....

> **TIP**
>
> Remember to make links between a business's marketing decisions and changes in the market by using examples from the case material.

Activity 12.2

This activity helps you to apply the theory of the product life cycle.

Creme Major is a well-established US-based medium-sized business renowned for its premium quality ice creams and frozen desserts. Creme Major has been successful in sustaining growth in both sales and profits over the last five years. One of the key strengths of Creme Major lies in its skilful management of the product life cycle. The business CEO, Sofia, and her management team have been good at managing a stream of new products to replace those in decline while positioning products in the maturity phase of the product life cycle to fund new products. Creme Major's marketing department has implemented extension strategies aimed at prolonging the life cycle of its products.

1 Define 'product life cycle'.

....

....

2 Outline **two** characteristics of the introduction phase of the product life cycle.

Try to set out what happens to sales and profits when Creme Major introduces new products.

....

....

....

....

3   Explain **two** extension strategies Creme Major might use to extend the mature stage of one of its brands.

    It is important to develop an example of an extension strategy, such as redesigning the product, and explain how this can maintain Creme Major's sales.

    ....

    ....

    ....

    ....

    ....

Activity 12.3

> This activity aims to help you understand the importance of a strong brand image as part of the marketing mix.

Gourmet Soups is a premium soup manufacturer based in Paraguay. The company produces high-quality organic soups using locally sourced ingredients, which it sells for a premium price. The business is committed to sustainability in all aspects of its operation and this is seen a key factor is making its brand so attractive. The company is always looking to promote the superior quality of its soups to its existing and potential customers. Gourmet Soups has a partnership with three local farms to ensure fresh, organic ingredients are used in its product. The company also invested in eco-friendly packaging to appeal to environmentally conscious consumers.

1   Outline **two** elements of Gourmet Soups marketing mix.

    You just need to describe two elements of the marketing mix here.

    ....

    ....

    ....

    ....

2   Explain **two** reasons why Gourmet Soups' commitment to sustainability might be of advantage to its business.

Try to make the link between sustainability and Gourmet Soups' brand image here.

....

....

....

....

....

....

3   Do you think the advantages to Gourmet Soups of using environmentally friendly packaging are greater than the disadvantages? Justify your answer.

Consider the advantages and disadvantages to Gourmet Soups of using environmentally friendly packaging. Evaluate by providing a justified decision as to whether the advantages are greater than the disadvantages to Gourmet Soups. Think about how using environmentally friendly packaging could impact Gourmet Soups costs or sales.

....

....

....

....

....

....

....

....

REFLECTION

Has your understanding of this topic improved as you have worked through the questions? Do you feel in a better position to answer future questions on the product element of the marketing mix? To improve further, speak to your teacher about elements of your answers that could done better.

Chapter 13
Marketing mix: price

LEARNING INTENTIONS

By the end of this chapter, you will be able to:

- identify pricing methods
- explain the advantages and disadvantages of pricing methods
- recommend which pricing strategy a business should use in a given situation.

KEY TERMS

competitive pricing   cost-plus pricing   dynamic pricing

penetration pricing   (price) skimming

Activity 13.1

This activity tests your knowledge of different pricing methods.

Table 13.1 sets out the characteristics of different pricing methods. Match the following pricing methods to their characteristics:

- skimming
- penetration pricing
- competitive pricing
- dynamic pricing
- cost-plus pricing.

Table 13.1: Examples of the different pricing methods used by businesses

Example	Pricing method
A plumbing firm calculates the cost of materials and labour for a job they are doing and then adds a percentage to set a final price to charge a customer.	
A mobile phone manufacturer sets an initially high price for a new mobile phone they are launching on the market.	
A pizza restaurant in a town looks at the prices other pizza restaurants are charging before it sets the prices for its pizzas.	
A taxi firm increases the price of its service during peak times.	
A fast food chain sets a low introductory price on a new 'meal deal' they have just introduced.	

Activity 13.2

> This activity tests your knowledge and understanding of different pricing methods.

Trans Global Airways is a long-haul airline that provides extensive flight services across various continents. Central to its marketing strategy is pricing, which is important in maximising both sales and profits. To appeal to consumers and increase sales, Trans Global Airways employs innovative pricing methods, focusing on attracting customers with competitive fares. However, the airline distinguishes itself by offering additional services such as insurance, car hire, hotel accommodations, fast-track boarding and seat selection with the hope of increasing the overall travel experience for passengers.

The finance director at Trans Global Airways, Anil, has an important role in deciding the company's pricing strategy. Anil believes it is important for the company's marketing department to think about the costs associated with providing services. By keeping a balance between having a competitive price in the market and the costs of providing the service, Trans Global Airways aims to have high revenues and offer good value to its customers.

1 Identify **four** factors that Trans Global Airways might consider when choosing a pricing method.

   You just need to list factors here.

   ....

   ....

   ....

   ....

2 Explain how Trans Global Airways might use cost plus pricing and competitive pricing when it is setting the price of its flights.

   Remember to think about the links Trans Global Airways has to make between the price it sets and the prices of its competitors and its promotional activity.

   ....

   ....

   ....

   ....

   ....

   ....

3 Explain **two** factors Trans Global Airway might consider when setting its price. Which factor do you think is the most important to Trans Global Airway? Justify your answer.

Consider two factors that might influence the price charged by Trans Global Airway and explain one advantage or disadvantage of each. Make a decision about which factor is the most important and explain why.

....

....

....

....

....

....

....

....

Activity 13.3

> This activity gets you to think about the importance of consumer demand in pricing decisions made by businesses.

The marketing team at Parque Aventura, a popular theme park in Columbia, is dedicated to maximising its sales revenue by implementing a pricing strategy based on different days and seasons. The director of marketing, Marco, aims to increase prices during weekends and national holidays when demand is high. On weekdays, however, when demand tends to be low, he proposes adjusting prices downward to attract more visitors.

1 Define 'revenue'.

....

....

2 Explain how an increase in Parque Aventura's price during the weekend leads to an increase in its revenues.

This question wants you to link pricing decisions and revenues.

....

....

....

....

REFLECTION

What key skills are necessary when you are analysing and evaluating pricing decisions made by businesses? How confident do you feel about applying these skills? Try doing as many questions as you can on this topic to increase your confidence.

> Chapter 14
Marketing mix: place

> **LEARNING INTENTIONS**
>
> By the end of this chapter, you will be able to:
> - identify different distribution channels
> - explain the advantages and disadvantages of different distribution channels
> - recommend an appropriate distribution channel for a business to use in a given situation.

> **KEY TERMS**
>
> channels of distribution   direct to consumers
>
> retailer   wholesaler

Activity 14.1

> This activity helps you to think about the different distribution channels that businesses use.

Crunchy Start is a German manufacturer of breakfast cereals such as muesli, oatmeal and cornflakes. It is a medium-sized family-owned company facing competition from large multinational food manufacturers. Effective distribution channels are an important part of Crunchy Start's success. The majority of its products are sold to customers through major supermarkets. The company also distributes its products through wholesalers, who sell them to small retailers. In addition, Crunchy Start directly sells its breakfast cereals to business customers such as hotels and cafes.

1 Define 'wholesaler'.

   ....

   ....

> **TIP**
>
> Make sure that you use precise terminology when you are defining a wholesaler. When you are answering 'define' questions, you need to use precise, accurate business terminology.

2 Outline the channel of distribution Crunchy Start uses when it sells to hotels and cafes.

Think about the different ways that a business can get its products to the customer and the intermediaries that the product will need to go through.

....

....

....

....

3 Explain **two** advantages to Crunchy Start of selling its breakfast cereals through major supermarkets.

Consider the advantages that wholesalers bring by buying goods in large quantities and selling those goods in smaller quantities to small businesses.

....

....

....

....

....

....

Activity 14.2

> **This activity helps you to understand the difference between physical retailing and online retailing.**

Nordic Elegance is an established shirt brand based in Sweden. Nordic Elegance's customers like the high quality of the shirts it produces and the original nature of their designs. Nordic Elegance has longstanding distribution links with prestigious department stores and boutique clothing retailers. The company has been slow to utilise online distribution directly to its consumers, but this is something the company's management has recently introduced.

1 Define 'direct to consumer.'

....

....

2 Outline the **two** methods of distribution Nordic Elegance is using.

Describe the ways the business gets its shirts to its customers.

....

....

....

....

3 Do you think the advantages to Nordic Elegance of selling directly to consumers are greater than the disadvantages? Justify your answer.

Consider the advantages and disadvantages to Nordic Elegance of selling direct to consumers. Evaluate by providing a justified decision as to whether the advantages to Nordic Elegance are greater than the disadvantages.

....

....

....

....

....

....

....

....

REFLECTION

Do you think the quality of your answers in this section has improved compared to earlier chapters? Are you getting better marks now than you were before? Discuss your progress with someone else in your class to see how much you have improved.

Chapter 15
Marketing mix: promotion

LEARNING INTENTIONS

By the end of this chapter, you will be able to:

- explain the reasons for promotion
- identify and explain methods of promotion and methods of advertising
- recommend methods of advertising and promotion for a business to use in given situations
- identify examples of ecommerce
- explain the advantages and disadvantages of ecommerce for businesses and for consumers.

KEY TERMS

advertising   ecommerce   promotion   sales promotion

Activity 15.1

This activity checks your knowledge of promotional methods.

Table 15.1 sets out examples of different methods of promotion.

Match each example with the following methods:

- sales promotion
- advertising

Table 15.1: The different methods of promotion used by businesses

Example	Method of promotion
A pizza delivery business sends information by post on price offers.	
A film distribution company sticks posters promoting its latest film on a city's subway system.	
A coffee shop offers customers a free cup of coffee each time they buy six cups of coffee.	

15 Marketing mix: promotion

Activity 15.2

This activity helps you to consider how different promotional methods and the marketing budget can have an impact on an organisation.

Peakpro manufactures outdoor wear and equipment. The company maintains a significant online presence and prefers direct sales to consumers rather than using retailers. It does, however, operate a limited number of branded stores. The directors are currently determining the marketing budget for the coming year and have budgeted to increase total advertising expenditure by 30% to expand Peakpro's market share. Peakpro recognises the importance of social media advertising in achieving this goal.

1   Outline **two** ways Peakpro could use social media advertising to increase its sales.

   Think about ways social media can be used to attract consumers to Peakpro's products.

   ....

   ....

   ....

   ....

2   Explain **two** disadvantages to Peakpro of selling its products directly to customers.

   Think about the challenges a business might face when trying to sell products online.

   ....

   ....

   ....

   ....

   ....

3   Explain **two** reasons why advertising is important to Peakpro. Which reason do you think is likely to be the most important? Justify your answer.

Explain two reasons why advertising is important to Peakpro. Evaluate by providing a justified decision as to the biggest reason why it is important to PeakPro.

....

....

....

....

....

....

....

....

Activity 15.3

> This activity helps you to consider how different ecommerce methods can be used by a business to promote its products and increase sales.

Stay-Down-Under is an online accommodation booking agency based in Australia. The company offers spaces in hotels and apartments in Australia for travellers from Australia and the rest of the world. Stay-Down-Under's promotional budget primarily focuses on online advertising and social media marketing. The effectiveness of the business's electronic booking and payment system is considered essential for its success in the market. However, the company has faced challenges in recent months due to security breaches in its system, resulting in unauthorised access and theft of payment information from some of its customers.

1   Outline **two** ways Stay-Down-Under can use ecommerce to promote its business.

Describe how mobile communication and the internet can be used by Stay-Down-Under.

....

....

....

....

15 Marketing mix: promotion

2 Explain **two** advantages to Stay-Down-Under of using ecommerce to sell spaces in hotels and apartments.

Think about the advantages to Stay-Down-Under of mobile communication and the internet to reach and communicate with customers.

....

....

....

....

3 Do you think the advantages to Stay-Down-Under of using social media to promote its products are greater than the disadvantages? Justify your answer.

Explain the advantages and disadvantages to Stay-Down-Under of using social media. Make a decision about whether the advantages are greater than the disadvantages, and justify your answer.

....

....

....

....

....

....

....

TIP
With 'explain' questions, you need to analyse by making links between business theory and outcome. For example, the way that social media advertising can increase a business's sales.

Activity 15.4

> This activity helps you think about the way businesses can use social media marketing to increase their sales.

Safaribeats is a summer music festival organiser located in South Africa. The company has experienced significant growth in recent years and has become a very profitable business. To continue to strengthen its brand image, the owners have appointed a new marketing director with a focus on modernising the Safaribeats brand. As part of its marketing strategy, the company plans to shift towards the use of social media as an important method of promotion. Safaribeats intends to attract some of the newest, well-known musical acts to improve the festival's reputation, despite the costs involved.

1 Identify **four** methods of promotion that Safaribeats might use.

   ....

   ....

   ....

   ....

2 Explain **two** advantages to Safaribeats of using social media advertising as a method of promotion.

   Remember how, for example, social media can target potential consumers very precisely.

   ....

   ....

   ....

   ....

   ....

   ....

REFLECTION

Think about what you have learnt about how businesses promote and distribute their products, considering how these strategies are influenced by the type of business being studied. To what extent has your understanding of advertising and sales promotion been improved? Look at the marks you are getting when you are answering questions on this topic to measure your improvement.

Chapter 16
Marketing strategy and legal controls

> **LEARNING INTENTIONS**
>
> By the end of this chapter, you should be able to:
>
> - understand marketing strategies
> - explain how legal controls influence marketing strategy
> - explain the advantages and disadvantages of entering new markets in other countries.

> **KEY TERM**
>
> marketing strategy

Activity 16.1

This activity is designed to check your understanding of marketing strategy.

Hot Press is a dry cleaning business that operates a chain of dry cleaning outlets in the Galician region of Spain. The business is planning to expand its operations into the Basque region. To achieve this, it needs to develop a marketing strategy. Hot Press has three key objectives that it wants to achieve:

- Generate annual revenue of $200 000 from each of the new outlets.
- Attain a market share of 20% after two years.
- Establish a unique selling point of 'quick and affordable cleaning'.

The key tactics for the Hot Press's strategy include investing in the latest dry cleaning equipment and ensuring that the staff is well trained.

1   Outline **two** elements of a marketing strategy.

    Describe the two elements of the marketing strategy you have chosen.

    ....

    ....

    ....

    ....

2   Identify the **four** elements of the marketing mix.

    You just need to list the elements of the marketing mix here.

    ....

    ....

    ....

    ....

3   Explain **two** advantages to Hot Press of having marketing objectives.

    Think about the effect that marketing objectives have on Hot Press' employees.

    ....

    ....

    ....

    ....

4   Do you think price or product is the most important element of Hot Press' marketing mix? Which element do you think is the most important? Justify your answer.

    Think about reasons why price and product are important elements of the marketing mix for Hot Press. Evaluate by providing a justified decision as to whether price or product is the most important element to Hot Press.

    ....

    ....

    ....

    ....

    ....

    ....

> **TIP**
>
> When you are answering marketing strategy questions, think about the methods businesses use to achieve their business objectives.

Activity 16.2

> Here, you are asked to look at the legal controls on business.

Pensa is an Italian business that sells tablet computers. The company is based in Milan, but its products are manufactured in Vietnam, and Pensa distributes them throughout Europe. Despite being equipped with the latest technology, there have been faults with the product, leading to a significant number of returns. Although Pensa has faced many challenges, its latest product has seen a significant increase in sales of over 30% this year. Pensa operates in a competitive market and faces strong competition from two established multinational competitors, which aim to drive Pensa out of the market through aggressive pricing strategies. The matter is currently under review by the competition authorities.

1 Identify **four** types of legal control that might affect a business's marketing strategy.

....

....

....

....

2 Outline **one** legal reason why Pensa would have to accept a returned faulty tablet computer.

Consider the laws that protect customers when they buy products.

....

....

3 Explain how the competition Pensa faces from the two multinational companies might be considered to be unfair.

Consider how a large company can use low prices to affect Pensa's position in the market.

....

....

....

4 Explain **two** ways legal controls over marketing can protect Pensa's customers. Which way do you think is likely to be the most important? Justify your answer.

Try to debate the advantages of controls for customers, such as production standards, against the problems of legal controls.

....

....

....

....

....

....

....

....

> **TIP**
>
> 'Justify' questions need you to show evaluative skills by looking at advantages and disadvantages of the point you are making.

Activity 16.3

This activity helps you to check your knowledge of the problems of entering new markets in other countries.

Table 16.1 sets out the problems of entering new markets in other countries.

Match each example with the following problems:

- differences in legal controls
- differences in language
- lack of market knowledge
- economic differences
- social differences.

16 Marketing strategy and legal controls

Table 16.1: Examples of the problems of entering new markets in other countries

Example	Problem
A confectionary manufacturer finds it difficult to sell its dark chocolate brand in another country because people tend not to eat dark chocolate in that country.	
The name of a brand of car has to be changed because the car's name does not translate well into the language of another country.	
A business sees its sales increase dramatically because of strong economic growth in one of its export markets.	
In its market research, a restaurant chain finds people like to eat earlier in the evening than they do in the restaurant chain's country of origin.	
An electrical goods manufacturer has to produce its kettles with safety lids in the country it plans to export to.	

Activity 16.4

> The objective of this activity is for you to examine the issues that a business faces when it enters an international market.

Bluegame is a Bulgarian board game manufacturer who is planning to export to a market in another country. Up to now, Bluegame has focused its sales efforts in Europe and North America but recognises the potential for growth in developing markets. However, entering the market in another country poses some challenges for Bluegame. The company lacks knowledge of customer preferences in the board game market of the target country, and there are significant trade barriers that it must overcome to establish itself in the market. Additionally, Bluegame has had to adapt its advertising and promotional methods to take into account language and cultural differences in the new market. Despite these challenges, Bluegame has the opportunity to gain market entry through a joint venture with a local board game manufacturer. This partnership would provide Bluegame with valuable insights into the local market, reduce entry barriers and streamline operations in the new market.

1   Define 'joint venture'.

    Use precise terminology when you are answering definition questions.

    ....

    ....

2   Outline **two** ways Bluegame might have to adapt its promotional methods when it enters the board game market in another country.

    Think about language and cultural issues when you are answering this question.

    ....

    ....

    ....

    ....

3   Explain **two** barriers Bluegame might encounter as it enters the board game market in another country.

    Do not forget to link the two barriers and how they will affect Bluegame's entry into the other country's board game market.

    ....

    ....

    ....

    ....

    ....

    ....

REFLECTION

Consider the insights you have gained on how businesses develop their marketing strategy and implement it to achieve their goals. Identify any specific areas where you could further improve your understanding of marketing strategy. Practising questions is a good way of doing this.

Section 3 Practice questions

Practice question 1

Velocity Gear sell sports clothing for men and women. It uses primary market research to make decisions about its marketing mix: price, product, promotion and place. Velocity Gear uses different methods of sales promotion to increase its sales. The Marketing Director has recently started using social media to advertise its products.

a   Identify **two** methods of primary market research. [2]

b   Outline **two** methods of sales promotion Velocity Gear could use. [4]

c   Explain **two** advantages to Velocity Gear of using social media to advertise its product. [6]

d   Which element of the marketing mix do you think is the most important for Velocity Gear? Justify your answer. [8]

Total available marks: 20

WORKED EXAMPLE

Question 1c
Model answer

Advantage 1: Low cost [K]. This can lead to more funds available to be spent elsewhere [An], such as for market research [Ap].

Advantage 2: Reaches many people [K]. This can lead to an increase in the potential number of sales [An] of sports clothing [Ap].

Improve this answer

Here is a sample answer to Practice question 1d. The answer contains common weaknesses. Read through this answer and consider how it could be improved.

Element 1: One element of the marketing mix is product [K]. This is sports clothing [Ap].

Element 2: Another element is promotion [K] to men and women [Ap].

Justification: I think that the most important element is product.

Your challenge

See whether you can improve this answer.

The answer provides two elements of the marketing mix and has made effective reference to the case study. However, there is no analysis for either of the elements. These points need to be developed to explain why each of the elements are an important part of the marketing mix. Think about what might happen if Velocity Gear did not make the right marketing decisions in each of these areas. The answer has made a decision but has not justified it in anyway therefore no evaluation was given. Think about which of these elements could be the most important and explain why.

CASE STUDY 1

FTR Gym

FTR Gym is a chain of fitness clubs in Country X that operates in the mass market. It has 80 gyms located across the country. The gym market has experienced significant growth over the last three years, although this growth has recently slowed down. This caused FTR Gym to conduct primary market research. The market research findings can be found in Appendix 1. FTR Gym carried out focus groups and a consumer survey.

FTR Gym uses lifestyle market research. The market is very competitive and the Managing Director is thinking about ways to increase the number of people who have memberships at the fitness clubs, or increase the number of people attending the fitness classes. Customers can either pay for a monthly membership or pay for individual classes. The Managing Director is thinking about developing new products such as offering new classes. He is also considering using methods of promotion such as loyalty card schemes and competitions. He is aware of legal controls related to marketing. FTR currently use a price skimming strategy. The Marketing Director thinks that it might be better to use penetration pricing or cost-plus pricing.

FTR Gym uses ecommerce in a range of different ways. Members can book and pay for classes online.

APPENDIX 1

FTR Gym market research

Key findings from the market research include:

'FTR gyms are expensive compared to competing gyms.'

'Some equipment in the gym is out of service for too long.'

'I think the gym could be open later in the evening.'

Section 3 Practice questions

1 a Explain **one** advantage and **one** disadvantage to FTR Gym of operating in a mass market.

Advantage:

Explanation:

Disadvantage:

Explanation: [8]

b Consider the following **three** changes that FTR Gym is considering to make based on the market research findings. Which change is likely to be the most beneficial to FTR Gym? Justify your answer.

Reducing its price:

Investing into new gym equipment:

Opening gyms later in the evenings:

Conclusion: [12]

2 a Explain **two** advantages to FTR Gym of using market segmentation.

Advantage 1:

Explanation:

Advantage 2:

Explanation: [8]

b Consider the following **two** methods of sales promotion that FTR Gym are considering introducing. Which method of promotion do you think FTR Gym should introduce? Justify your answer.

Competitions:

A loyalty card scheme:

Conclusion: [12]

3 a Explain **two** advantages to FTR Gym of developing new products.

Advantage 1:

Explanation:

Advantage 2:

Explanation: [8]

b Consider the advantages and disadvantages to FTR Gym of using the following **two** pricing methods. Which pricing method should FTR Gym use? Justify your answer.

Cost plus pricing:

Penetration pricing:

Conclusion: [12]

BUSINESS FOR CAMBRIDGE IGCSE™ AND O LEVEL: WORKBOOK

4 a Explain **two** legal controls related to marketing that FTR Gym will need to consider.

Legal control 1:

Explanation:

Legal control 2:

Explanation: [8]

b Consider the advantages and disadvantages to FTR Gym of using ecommerce in the following **two** ways. Which way do you think is the most important for FTR Gym? Justify your answer.

Electronic payment:

Online class reservation:

Conclusion: [12]

Total available marks: 80

WORKED EXAMPLE

Question 1a

1 a Advantage: Higher levels of sales [**K**].

Explanation: This can lead to an increase in the potential revenue gained by FTR Gym [**An**]. This is because they are likely to have more gym members [**Ap**] than a niche market business. This could lead to an increase in market share [**An**].

Disadvantage: There are high levels of competition [**K**].

Explanation: This could lead to high levels of promotion and advertising being required [**An**]. This can increase costs for the business [**An**]. This can leave fewer funds available for other activities such as market research [**Ap**].

Improve this answer

Here is a sample answer to Case study question 1b. The answer contains some common weaknesses. Read each part and consider how the answer could be improved.

b   Reducing prices: If FTR Gym reduces its prices then this could lead to an increase in sales [K]. More customers might purchase gym memberships [Ap]. This can increase total revenue.

Investment in new gym equipment: This can improve the quality of the experience for members [K]. As a result this could improve the reputation of the business [An], which could attract new customers [An].

Opening gyms later in the evenings: This can lead to the needs of a wider range of members being met, and may possibly appeal to an entirely new group of customers [K]. This can increase revenue streams [An].

Conclusion: The most beneficial change would be to reduce prices. As the market growth has slowed down this is likely to attract more customers as the memberships will be more affordable [E].

Your challenge

See whether you can improve this answer.

This answer has a good range of points made, and some relevant application. There is also some relevant development of the knowledge points. However, for each of the changes being considered, there are only advantages provided in the discussion. Disadvantages for each change need to be discussed. Without a balanced discussion, it is hard to offer a justified decision. The conclusion also identifies reduce prices to be the most beneficial. However, there is no rejection of an alternative change.

Section 4
Operations management

> Chapter 17
Production of goods and services

LEARNING INTENTIONS

By the end of this chapter, you will be able to:

- explain the production process
- explain why businesses need to hold inventories
- understand the concept of productivity, know how to calculate productivity, the benefits of increasing efficiency and identify ways to increase efficiency
- identify production methods and explain their advantages and disadvantages
- understand how technology influences production methods
- explain ways businesses can be more sustainable.

KEY TERMS

batch production   flow production   inventory   job production

labour productivity   lean production   production

Activity 17.1

In this activity, you will need to consider the nature of production and productivity in an organisation.

Tun Air manufactures light aircraft that are distributed globally. As the market leader in the industry, Tun Air holds a dominant market share of 31% in the global market for light aircraft. The company's most successful manufacturing facility is in Tunisia, boasting the highest level of labour productivity among all light aircraft manufacturers worldwide.

The Tunisian plant operates very efficiently, producing 200 light aircraft a year while employing a workforce of 250 highly skilled individuals. Tun Air thinks the success of this facility to its well-trained and motivated employees, who are equipped with the latest technological advancements in the production line. This combination of skilled personnel and cutting-edge technology ensures that Tun Air maintains its position as a leader in the light aircraft manufacturing industry.

17 Production of goods and services

1 Define 'labour productivity'.

Be precise in your use of terminology here.

....

....

2 State the equation used to measure labour productivity.

....

....

> **TIP**
>
> For this 'state' question, you just need to set out the equation used to calculate productivity.

3 Calculate Tun Air's labour productivity.

Make sure you show your working here.

....

....

4 Explain **two** advantages to Tun Air of having well-trained employees. Which advantage do you think is likely to be the most important to Tun Air? Justify your answer.

Think about the link between an employee's skill level and their productivity.

....

....

....

....

....

....

....

Activity 17.2

> **This activity will help you to demonstrate your understanding of inventory management.**

The new operations director, Celia, at the large Spanish furniture retail chain, Furnishista, aims to increase operational efficiency. One area of focus for Furnishista is inventory management. Celia believes that the company maintains excessive inventory levels of all types of furniture, which creates operational difficulties in Furnishista's stores. By reducing inventory levels, she anticipates cost savings and increased profitability for the company.

1 Define 'inventory'.

   ....

   ....

2 Outline **two** costs associated with holding inventories.

   You need to think about and set out the costs of holding inventories.

   ....

   ....

   ....

   ....

3 Explain **two** benefits to Furnishista of holding inventory.

   It is important to make the link between the advantages of holding inventory and then analyse this by showing its positive implications for Furnishista.

   ....

   ....

   ....

   ....

   ....

   ....

Activity 17.3

> Here, you must show your knowledge and understanding of lean production.

Luis is the owner of a Uruguayan surfboard manufacturing company called Wax and Wave that has successfully implemented lean production techniques over the past two years, leading to a significant increase in the business's profits. The important parts of this change included adopting just-in-time inventory control and incorporating Kaizen principles into the manufacturing process. Wax and Wave has a skilled and motivated workforce that quickly adapted to the use of lean production, contributing to the company's success in producing high-quality surfboards efficiently.

1   Define 'just-in-time inventory control'.

    Think about using the right terminology when you do this definition question.

    ....

    ....

2   Identify **four** reasons for waste in a business such as Wax and Wave.

    Remember you just need to list four points here.

    ....

    ....

    ....

    ....

3   Outline **two** characteristics of 'Kaizen principles' Wax and Wave might use when it is manufacturing its surfboards.

    Think about the way Kaizen is used in the production process and the way it affects employees.

    ....

    ....

    ....

    ....

4 Explain **two** reasons why the introduction of lean production might have increased Wax and Wave's profits.

Think about the way lean production might affect Wax and Wave's costs and revenues.

....

....

....

....

....

....

Activity 17.4

> The aim of this activity is to check your knowledge and understanding of sustainable production.

In response to growing environmental concerns and consumer demands for eco-friendly products, Alma Cosmetics, a leading manufacturer of cosmetics products in Thailand, has started to use sustainable production methods in its operations. Alma Cosmetics faced several challenges in changing to sustainable production methods, including higher initial investment costs, resistance to change from some employees and the need to change some of its suppliers.

1 Define 'production'.

....

....

2 Explain **two** ways Alma Cosmetics could be more sustainable in the way it manufactures its products.

Think how Alma Cosmetics needs to change the resources it uses to be more sustainable.

....

....

....

....

17 Production of goods and services

3   Do you think Alma Cosmetics should change to more sustainable production? Justify your answer.

Start this answer by explaining the benefits to Alma Cosmetics of using more sustainable production methods. Evaluate your answer by considering the disadvantages.

....

....

....

....

....

....

Activity 17.5

In this activity, you will need to apply your knowledge and understanding of different production methods.

La Poteries Francaise is a well-known pottery manufacturer that has a reputation for its high levels of efficiency and productivity. The company uses batch production methods in its pottery production plants, where it produces a wide range of household ceramic products such as dinnerware sets. La Poteries Francaise also operates a dedicated pottery studio specialising in making custom pieces for special events and occasions. This studio employs job production techniques that handmakes individual pieces tailored to meet the specific needs and preferences of customers.

1   Outline the difference between batch production and job production.

Use precise terminology to show the differences between batch production and job production.

....

....

....

....

2 Explain **two** reasons why La Poteries Francaise uses job production in certain situations.

   Consider the customers' needs when La Poteries Francaise is using job production.

   ....

   ....

   ....

   ....

   ....

   ....

3 Do you think the advantages to La Poteries Francaise of using batch production are greater than the disadvantages? Justify your answer.

   Consider the advantages and disadvantages to La Poteries Francaise of using batch production.

   ....

   ....

   ....

   ....

   ....

   ....

   ....

Activity 17.6

This activity covers the ways that technology affects production.

Cooking Solutions is a Portuguese manufacturer of commercial ovens. The business has recently established a new production facility in South America, which began operations six months ago. Cooking Solutions employs up to date technology in its new plant, incorporating advanced computer-aided manufacturing (CAM) and 3D printing. The implementation of this technology has resulted in a 20% reduction in the workforce employed by Cooking Solutions, leading to a significant decrease in the company's unit costs.

1. Identify **two** ways technology can be used in production by Cooking Solutions.

   ....

   ....

   ....

   ....

2. Explain **two** ways the use of technology might have increased Cooking Solutions productivity.

   Think about the link between the use of technology and 3D printing and how it might increase business efficiency.

   ....

   ....

   ....

   ....

   ....

   ....

3   Explain **two** advantages to Cooking Solutions of using technology. Which advantage do you think is likely to be the most important to Cooking Solutions? Justify your answer.

Consider the advantages to Cooking Solutions of using technology. Evaluate by providing a justified decision as to which reason is likely to be the most important to Cooking Solutions.

....

....

....

....

....

....

....

....

REFLECTION

You have had the opportunity to do plenty of activity questions in this chapter. Do you feel your answers to these types of questions is improving? Have you changed your approach to improve your answers? Have you responded positively to the advice of your teacher?

> Chapter 18
Costs, scale of production and break-even analysis

LEARNING INTENTIONS

By the end of this chapter, you will be able to:

- identify the different classification of business costs and provide examples for these
- explain the usefulness of cost data in business decision-making
- explain economies and diseconomies of scale
- explain the concept of break-even, and be able to interpret, amend and complete a break-even chart
- explain the margin of safety
- calculate break-even and margin of safety
- explain the limitations of break-even analysis.

KEY TERMS

average total cost   break-even   diseconomies of scale

economies of scale   fixed cost   margin of safety   total cost

total variable cost   variable cost per unit

Activity 18.1

In this activity, you will be required to demonstrate what you have learnt about fixed and variable costs.

Table 18.1 sets out the costs of a business that manufactures shoes. Classify the costs listed as either fixed costs or variable costs.

Table 18.1: Examples of fixed and variable costs

Example of cost	Fixed or variable cost
Insurance on the firm's building	
Leather used to produce the firm's shoes	
Salary of the CEO	
Packaging used for the shoes	
The material used to produce shoelaces	
Rent of the company's buildings	
Production line workers' wages on piece rates	

Activity 18.2

This question helps to develop your understanding of the relationship between costs and output using cost data.

As a high-quality table manufacturer, Tablecraft is a small, family-run business that supplies premium tables to restaurants. Table 18.2 shows the cost data for the business:

Table 18.2: Cost data for Tablecraft

Output	Fixed cost	Variable cost $160 per table	Total cost $	Average cost $
0	800 000			
5000				
10 000				
15 000				
20 000				
25 000				

1   Outline the difference between a fixed cost and a variable cost.

   Explain why knowing how fixed and variable costs are affected by ouput.

   ....

   ....

   ....

   ....

2 Calculate the fixed, variable, total and average costs at each level of output by completing the table.

You need to work out cost values from the given figures.

Be clear on your method for calculating the different costs and think about how realistic your cost figures are relative to the case study example.

....

....

....

....

3 Explain **two** reasons why average cost is useful to Tablecraft.

Think about the impact of fixed costs when calculating average costs.

....

....

....

....

....

....

Activity 18.3

This activity helps to develop your understanding of how variable costs affect break-even and margin of safety.

Pintura Pictures is a Uruguay-based business that manufactures printed pictures to sell to furniture retailers. The pictures are reprints of famous paintings and photographs that customers can use to decorate their homes. The business has a break-even output of 7 000 units and a margin of safety of 2 000 units. Pintura Pictures is trying to reduce its variable costs by negotiating a lower price for its raw materials with a new supplier. While this could reduce the business's break-even point, there are some concerns that the new supplier's materials are not of the same quality as its existing supplier's.

1 Define 'break-even'.

   ....

   ....

2 Outline what Pintura Pictures' break-even output of 7000 units and margin of safety of 2000 units means.

   You need to describe break-even output and margin of safety.

   ....

   ....

   ....

   ....

3 Explain why a lower price for the raw materials Pintura Pictures buys might reduce its break-even output.

   Try to make the link between variable costs and break-even output.

   ....

   ....

   ....

   ....

Activity 18.4

> **The aim of this activity is for you to show your knowledge of the different types of economies of scale.**

Table 18.3 sets out examples of different **economies of scale**.

Complete the table by matching the examples with the following types of economies of scale:

- technical
- financial
- managerial
- purchasing
- marketing.

Table 18.3: Examples of types of economies of scale

Example	Type of economies of scale
A sportswear manufacturer can secure a loan at a low rate of interest.	
A shipping company uses larger vessels to move its containers.	
A supermarket chain can allocate managers to different departments.	
A car manufacturer buys components in large quantities.	
A confectionary manufacturer divides its promotion budget across a large sales volume.	

Activity 18.5

This activity is designed to help you to practise your skills in applying the break-even model.

Satellite Education provides educational courses and training programs for various industries. Over the past five years, the company has experienced substantial growth, leading to economies of scale that have lowered the average cost of delivering educational services. However, with this growth, Satellite Education is facing challenges related to communication and coordination among its teams. Figure 18.1 illustrates the break-even output and the current level of output for Satellite Education.

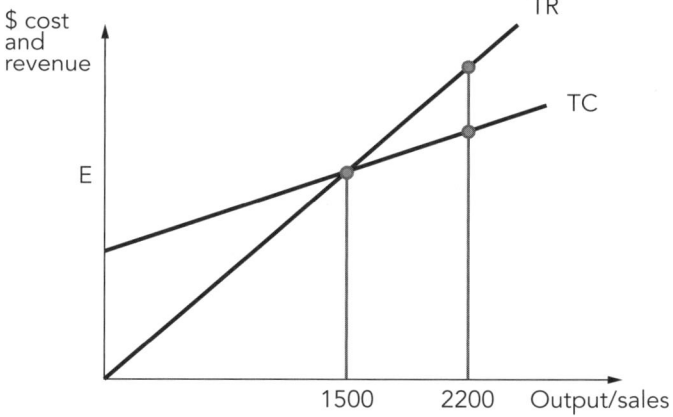

Figure 18.1: Break-even output and the current level of output for Satellite Education

BUSINESS FOR CAMBRIDGE IGCSE™ AND O LEVEL: WORKBOOK

1 Define 'margin of safety'.

Make sure you use precise terminology here.

....

....

2 Outline the difference between purchasing and financial economies of scale.

Remember to think about the cost advantages of being a larger business.

....

....

....

....

3 Using the break-even diagram, identify the break-even output and calculate the margin of safety.

Remember to show your working for this calculate question.

....

....

....

....

4 Do you think the advantages to Satellite Education of using break-even analysis are greater than the disadvantages? Justify your answer.

Consider the reasons why break-even analysis is advantageous and disadvantageous for Satellite Education. Evaluate by providing a justified decision as to whether the advantages are greater than the disadvantages.

....

....

....

....

18 Costs, scale of production and break-even analysis

....

....

....

REFLECTION

Has your understanding of this topic improved as you have worked your way through the chapter? Have the marks you have achieved on the questions you have answered improved? Discuss the work you have done on this topic with someone else in your class so you can improve further.

Chapter 19
Quality of goods and services

LEARNING INTENTIONS

By the end of this chapter, you will be able to:

- explain why quality is important to businesses
- understand the concept of quality control and explain its advantages and disadvantages
- understand the concept of quality assurance and explain its advantages and disadvantages.

KEY TERMS

quality assurance	quality control

Activity 19.1

This activity introduces you to quality and why it is important.

Frame-it manufactures and sells custom-made picture frames through its online platform. Customers use the company's innovative software to design their ideal frames, which are promptly delivered within four days. The company is known for its high product quality and has established a high market share. Frame-it uses state-of-the-art technology throughout its business and this allows it to achieve very high product quality. One issue the company faces is making sure customers clearly understand the ordering software they use to design their frames.

1   Identify **two** indicators of poor quality.

   Make sure you use precise terminology in your definition.

   ....

   ....

2   Outline **two** ways Frame-it can use quality control to achieve high-quality standards.

   Think about the importance of labour and capital in affecting Frame-it's quality standards.

   ....

   ....

19 Quality of goods and services

....

....

3 Explain how the issue of the 'ordering software' might affect Frame-it's quality.

Think about the importance of precise ordering in affecting the final product Frame-it produces.

....

....

....

....

4 Explain **two** reasons why quality is important to Frame-it. Which reason do you think is likely to be the most important to Frame-it? Justify your answer.

Explain two reasons why quality might be important to Frame-it. Make a justified decision as to which reason you think is likely to be the most important.

....

....

....

....

....

....

....

> **TIP**
>
> Remember to include references to the case study in your answer to part 4 of this question. This will show your understanding of the topic and your ability to apply business theory.

Activity 19.2

> This activity tests your understanding of quality and how it affects business performance.

There are challenges at the Blossom Boutique Hotel. Over the past year, both sales and profits have seen a significant decline due to a decrease in customer satisfaction. Many customer complaints come from poor quality service and poor quality food. In the last two years, the management at Blossom Boutique Hotel has cut costs by hiring inexperienced lower-wage staff. There are also concerns about poor management, which has had a bad effect on staff morale. Unfortunately, this decision has led to a decline in staff motivation.

1   Outline **two** indicators of poor quality standards at Blossom Boutique Hotel.

    Think about factors that affect standards that meet the needs of Blossom Boutique Hotel's customers.

    ....

    ....

    ....

    ....

2   Explain **two** reasons why a decline in quality at Blossom Boutique Hotel might have led to a decline in sales.

    It is important to think about the way a fall in quality affects customer demand.

    ....

    ....

    ....

    ....

    ....

    ....

Activity 19.3

> **The aim of this activity is to help you check your understanding of quality control.**

Sonic Sound Systems manufactures high-end speakers that are fitted and sold at premium prices. Quality is a key feature of the business because its customers are willing to pay a premium for the highest standards of performance and craftsmanship.

Over the past two years, Sonic Sound Systems has encountered several quality issues, putting pressure on the manager of the quality control department. There is a belief within the company that it should change from quality control to quality assurance. The management at Sonic Sound Systems believes the switch to quality assurance will prevent defects and ensure consistent quality across all its speaker models.

The switch from quality control to quality assurance involves investing in advanced testing technologies, enhancing production processes and using strict quality management systems.

1   Outline the difference between quality control and quality assurance.

   Remember to use precise terminology when you are answering this outline question.

   ....

   ....

   ....

   ....

2   Explain **two** problems for Sonic Sound Systems in using quality control.

   Think about the problems of measuring quality only at certain moments in the production process.

   ....

   ....

   ....

   ....

   ....

   ....

> **TIP**
>
> This 'explain' question asks you to set out the relationships and reasons why and how quality control might adversely affect Sonic Sound Systems.

3   Explain **two** advantages to Sonic Sound Systems of using quality assurance. Which advantage do you think is likely to be the most important to Sonic Sound Systems? Justify your answer.

Think about the advantages to Sonic Sound Systems of using quality assurance.

....

....

....

....

....

....

....

Activity 19.4

> This activity gets you to show your evaluative skills and understanding of quality assurance.

The decision to implement quality assurance at Solarlite by CEO Anil is seen as a key reason for the company's 15% increase in profits. Solarlite is a Moroccan company that sells manufacturing and installing solar panels. The introduction of quality assurance has brought important production benefits to Solarlite. As a result, the solar panels they produce have significantly fewer faults, leading to substantial cost reductions for the company and improved customer satisfaction.

1   Identify **four** elements of quality assurance.

You just need to list your points here.

....

....

....

....

2 Explain why the use of quality assurance by Solarlite might have led to a rise in customer satisfaction.

Try to make the link between quality assurance and how Solarlite's customers feel about the business's products.

....

....

....

....

....

....

REFLECTION

Do you feel more confident about answering questions of this topic? Do you feel answering the questions improves your confidence? Try discussing your answer with your teacher to further improve your confidence.

> Chapter 20
Location decisions

> **LEARNING INTENTIONS**
>
> By the end of this chapter, you will be able to:
>
> - explain the factors influencing the location decision of manufacturing and service businesses
>
> - explain why businesses may decide to locate their operations in another country, and identify the factors that would influence the choice of country to locate in.

Activity 20.1

> **This activity develops your understanding of how location decisions are made by businesses.**

A critical decision for Tab Technology is determining the best location for its new tablet computer manufacturing plant in Tanzania. Tab Technology's management believes that locating in an urban centre in the country is crucial for the company's future success. Establishing the new plant will allow Tab Technology to increase its production capacity by 50%. The port city of Dar es Salaam in Tanzania is considered an advantageous location due to its port location, cost-effective site and access to a skilled local workforce. However, there are some location concerns about traffic congestion in the port area and how that impacts the Tab Technology's employees and the distribution of its products.

1   Explain how the port location might affect Tab Technology's location decision.

   Make the link between, for example, the port location and Tab Technology's access to international markets.

   ....

   ....

   ....

   ....

   ....

2 How important do you think access to a skilled labour force is in Tab Technology's location decision?

   Think about the benefits of accessing a skilled labour force to Tab Technology. Try to evaluate this by considering other factors that might affect the business's location decision.

   ....

   ....

   ....

   ....

   ....

   ....

Activity 20.2

This activity develops your understanding of how a location to another country is decided upon.

Expanding into markets in another country is a significant decision for Micronova, a manufacturer of microwave ovens. The company's CEO, Sofia, believes that establishing a new manufacturing facility in Turkey is crucial for Micronova's future expansion. A potential location in Turkey is the country's capital, Istanbul. This location offers some notable advantages such as an available labour force, well-developed infrastructure, government grants, low regulation and the potential to export to other markets across Southern Europe. Turkey's high inflation rate does, however, make certain aspects of locating in the country difficult.

1 Identify **two** reasons why a business might locate in another country.

   You just need to list your points here.

   ....

   ....

2 Outline how support from the government and available labour might affect Micronova's location decision.

   Remember to describe how these two factors might affect Micronova's location decision.

   ....

   ....

BUSINESS FOR CAMBRIDGE IGCSE™ AND O LEVEL: WORKBOOK

....

....

3   Explain how good quality road connections and an available labour force might benefit Micronova if it is located in Istanbul.

Make links between developed infrastructure and the available labour force and the gains it might bring to Micronova.

....

....

....

....

....

....

....

> **TIP**
>
> When you are answering this 'explain' question, you need to consider the implications for Micronova of good quality road connections and an available labour force.

4   Explain **two** factors that might have influenced Micronova's location decision. Which factor do you think is likely to be the most important to Micronova? Justify your answer.

Explain two factors that may affect the location decision of Micronova and evaluate by making a justified decision as to which is likely to be the most important to the business.

....

....

....

....

....

....

....

Activity 20.3

> This activity develops your understanding of how workers are affected when a company moves to another country.

Create Comm Advertising has made the strategic decision to move their operations from Brussels, Belgium, to Copenhagen, Denmark. While this move promises exciting opportunities for growth and expansion, it also comes with challenges that need to be addressed. Many employees at Create Comm are concerned about locating in another country, and the agency recognises the importance of ensuring their well-being during the change period. Additionally, there are legal controls associated with the move, particularly regarding work visas for some employees who will need to obtain proper authorisation to work in Denmark. Furthermore, securing an office in Copenhagen has presented challenges due to Danish commercial property regulations. Create Comm remains committed to establishing its presence in Copenhagen and wants a successful change for its employees and operations.

1   Identify **four** functional areas of business that might be affected by a business's location in another country.

   You just need to make a list here.

   ....

   ....

   ....

   ....

2   Outline **two** challenges Create Comm might face when it locates its staff in another country.

   Think about the way workers might be affected if they must move to work in another country.

   ....

   ....

   ....

   ....

3 Explain how locating Create Comm employees to Copenhagen might increase the business's productivity.

Consider how a new location might improve the working conditions of Create Comm's workforce.

....

....

....

....

....

....

REFLECTION

Consider all the factors that affect business location and what you have learnt about them. Which factors are you confident about explaining and which do you find more difficult? How do you think you can improve the way you explain things?

Section 4 Practice questions

Practice question 1

Austoys manufactures children's toys using flow production. Its target market is children between four and eight years of age. Austoys uses just-in-time inventory control. The Finance Director is using cost and revenue data to calculate the break-even level of output for Austoys. This cost and revenue data is summarised in Table 1. Austoys is thinking about expanding its operations and opening another factory in Country X. There are many factors affecting the location decision.

Table 1: Summary of Austoys' cost and revenue data

Cost and revenue	$
Fixed cost	140 000
Variable cost (per toy)	8
Selling price (per toy)	22

The new manufacturing plant in Country X will use computer-aided manufacturing and just-in-time inventory management.

a Calculate Austoys break-even level of output. [2]

b Identify **four** factors that could influence the location decision of a manufacturing business. [4]

c Explain **two** advantages to Austoys of using flow production. [6]

d Do you think the advantages of Austoys using just-in-time inventory control are greater than the disadvantages? Justify your answer. [8]

Total available marks: [20]

WORKED EXAMPLE

Question 1c

Advantage 1: Can benefit from economies of scale [**K**]. This can lower the average cost [**An**] for the toy manufacturer [**Ap**].

Advantage 2: A high level of output can be produced [**K**]. This can make it more likely to meet customer demands [**An**] for children between four and eight years of age [**Ap**].

Improve this answer

Here is a sample answer to Practice question 1d. The answer contains some weaknesses. Read through this answer and consider how it could be improved.

Using just-in-time inventory control can reduce the amount of cash tied up in inventory [K]. This can help to improve the liquidity [An] of the toy manufacturer [Ap].

Justification: I think that the advantages of just in time are greater than the disadvantages for Austoys as improved liquidity makes it more likely that it can continue to pay its suppliers, which can improve relationships. This may make it easier for Austoys to negotiate for quick delivery in times of sudden changes in demand [E].

Your challenge

See whether you can improve this answer. The answer starts well and includes a well explained benefit of just-in-time inventory control that is in context of the business. However, no disadvantages are provided. A disadvantage should be identified and explained in context of Austoys. This will allow for a justified decision to be made. The advantages and disadvantages can be considered before a decision is made as to whether the advantages are greater than the disadvantages. Use the judgement given to provide and explain a relevant disadvantage of just-in-time inventory control.

CASE STUDY 1

Kirseaer has ten hotels in Country X. It is a hotel chain that offers affordable prices for leisure and business travellers. Kirseaer is a sustainable business. It re-uses products where possible and reduces waste where possible. Kirsear is expanding its business by opening another hotel in Country X. There are a range of factors affecting the location decision of the new hotel. One of the reasons the Managing Director wants to expand the business is so that it can benefit from economies of scale such as purchasing economies and marketing economies.

Kirseaer is looking into how to improve the quality of service offered in its hotels. It is thinking about the advantages and disadvantages of quality control and quality assurance. It employs experienced managers who are paid high salaries. Kirseaer is trying to increase efficiency at the hotel by training its workers and using technology to check-in hotel guests.

Kirseaer uses lean production to minimise waste. It currently uses a just-in-time inventory control system for items such as food for its restaurant, and cleaning suppliers used to clean the hotel. The Managing Director is thinking about introducing Kaizen.

Table 1 summarises cost, price and sales data for one of Kirseaer's hotels.

Appendix 1

Table 1: Summary of cost, revenue and sales data for one of Kirseaer's hotels

Cost, revenue and sales data for one hotel	
Fixed cost	$400 000
Selling price	$150
Variable cost	$70
Rooms sold	6000

1 a Explain **two** advantages to Kirseaer of using just-in-time inventory control.

Advantage 1:

Explanation:

Advantage 2:

Explanation: **[8]**

b Consider the advantages and disadvantages to Kirseaer of the following **two** methods of checking quality. Which method do you think is the best for Kirseaer to use? Justify your answer.

Quality control:

Quality assurance:

Conclusion: **[12]**

2 a Using the information in Appendix 1:

  i calculate Kirseaer's break-even level of output **[2]**

  ii calculate Kirseaer's margin of safety **[2]**

  iii identify **four** benefits of calculating the margin of safety.

  Benefit 1:

  Benefit 2:

  Benefit 3:

  Benefit 4: **[4]**

b Consider the advantages and disadvantages to Kirseaer of the following **two** methods of increase efficiency of its employees. Which method is likely to be the most effective for Kirsear? Justify your answer.

Training employees:

Using technology to check in hotel guests:

Conclusion: **[12]**

3   a   Explain **two** factors that might affect Kirseaer's location decision for its new hotel.

Factor 1:

Explanation:

Factor 2:

Explanation: [8]

   b   Consider the following **two** economies of scale that Kirseaer might benefit from as it grows in size. Which economy of scale do you think is the most important to Kirseaer? Justify your answer.

Purchasing economies of scale:

Marketing economies of scale:

Conclusion: [12]

4   a   Explain **two** advantages to Kirseaer of being sustainable.

Advantage 1:

Explanation:

Advantage 2:

Explanation: [8]

   b   Consider the advantages and disadvantages to Kirseaer of the following **two** methods of becoming more sustainable. Which method is likely to be most important to Kirseaer? Justify your answer.

Re-use:

Reducing waste:

Conclusion: [12]

Total marks available: 80

Section 4 Practice questions

> **WORKED EXAMPLE**
>
> ## Question 3b
>
> Purchasing economies of scale: As the hotel grows in size it is likely to buy greater quantities of raw materials. This means that the business is more likely to be able to negotiate discounts from suppliers if they are buying in bulk [**K**]. This can lead to a reduction in average costs [**An**], which could lead to lower prices being charged [**An**]. This is important to Kirsear as they are a hotel that offers rooms at affordable prices [**Ap**]. However, there is no guarantee that suppliers will offer a discount, or the business may have to use a different supplier instead to get the discount [**K**]. The new supplier may offer a lower quality of materials which could decrease the quality of service offered [**An**].
>
> Marketing economies of scale: As the business grows in size, its marketing costs do not rise at the same rate as its sales. This means that a business can spread its marketing costs over a greater number of sales [**K**], which reduces the average cost of marketing [**An**]. However, the new hotel may require significant marketing as it first opens [**K**] so there may be a delay before Kirseaer benefits from this economy of scale, meaning no immediate reduction in average costs [**An**].
>
> Conclusion: I think that purchasing economies of scale are likely to be the most important. The greater the volume of purchase from the supplier, the more power the business has. The supplier is unlikely to want to lose Kirsear as a customer therefore the hotel is more likely to negotiate a discount. Marketing is less important as the cost of marketing the new hotel may be quite significant, especially if there are competitors in the area [**E**].

Improve this answer

Here is a sample answer to Case study question 3a. Read through this answer and consider how it could be improved.

Factor 1: The size of the site [**K**].

Explanation: Without a big enough site, Kirseaer will struggle to meet customer demand [**An**].

Factor 2: How close the site is to suppliers [**K**].

Explanation: The business will need to make sure that it can continue to use just-in-time inventory control [**Ap**].

Your challenge

See whether you can improve this answer.

Factor 1: There is a valid knowledge point identified here, however, there is no application in this answer. There is also some development, but not enough to cover the two points needed for this factor.

Factor 2: Again, there is a valid knowledge point with good reference to the case study. However, there is no development at all of these points meaning no analysis is given for this factor.

Section 5
Financial information and decisions

Chapter 21
Business finance

> **LEARNING INTENTIONS**
>
> By the end of this chapter, you will be able to:
> - understand why businesses need finance
> - understand the difference between short- and long-term finance
> - understand and calculate working capital
> - identify and explain the main internal and external sources of finance
> - understand the advantages and disadvantages of internal and external sources of finance
> - outline the main factors to consider when selecting a source of finance
> - recommend and justify an appropriate source of finance for a given situation.

> **KEY TERMS**
>
> bank loan   crowdfunding   current assets   current liabilities
> hire purchase   leasing   liquidity   non-current assets   overdraft
> retained profit   share issue   trade receivables
> venture capital   working capital

Activity 21.1

> **This activity will help you to apply your understanding of why businesses need finance.**

One year ago, Olga left her job in insurance and started On-the-Square Coffee, her own 'pop-up' coffee shop, in a main square in Amsterdam. Olga invested $40 000 of her own savings and secured a $50 000 bank loan as an initial investment into her new business. Her start-up costs involved purchasing a high-quality stall and a coffee machine and setting up a computer system for managing transactions. In addition, she allocated funds for purchasing coffee beans and other ingredients.

1. Identify **four** reasons why businesses need finance.

   You just need to list the reasons here.

   ....

   ....

2   Define 'start-up capital'.

    Remember to be precise when you are defining terms.

    ....

    ....

3   Outline the difference between interest payments and loan repayments on the $50 000 bank loan Olga has taken out.

    Think about the ongoing cost of any loan when it is taken out by Olga.

    ....

    ....

    ....

    ....

4   Explain **two** advantages to Olga of using her own savings as a source of finance. Which advantage do you think is likely to be the most important to Olga? Justify your answer.

    Consider the advantages to Olga of using her own savings as a source of finance and evaluate by providing a justified decision as to the most important advantage to Olga.

    ....

    ....

    ....

    ....

    ....

    ....

    ....

Activity 21.2

> This activity helps you to consider the types of finance that businesses can use.

It has been a very strong year for Viva Naranja Citrus Farm in Spain. Over the past 12 months, revenue has increased by 25%, with profits experiencing a 22% increase. With this success, Viva Naranja is presented with the chance to acquire a new farm located 10 miles away, effectively doubling the farm's capacity. The $2 million expense of the new farm will be partly covered by retained profits and partly through a mortgage. However, the farm is concerned about the high interest expenses linked to the mortgage. The business already has significant interest payments on its short-term finance.

1. Define 'long-term finance'.

   ....

   ....

2. Identify **two** types of short-term finance.

   ....

   ....

3. Do you think the advantages to Viva Naranja of using retained profit as a source of finance are greater than the disadvantages? Justify your answer.

   Explain the advantages and disadvantages to Viva Naranja of using retained profits as a source of finance. Evaluate by providing a justified decision as to whether the advantages are greater than the disadvantages.

   ....

   ....

   ....

   ....

   ....

   ....

   ....

> **TIP**
>
> This 'justify' question is asking you to have a discussion that leads to a conclusion on whether Viva Naranja should use retained profits.

21 Business finance

Activity 21.3

> Here, you are expected to answer questions on funding for a small business.

Establishing a presence in the Pakistani clothing market was a challenge for Trendy Tees, a small retailer of T-shirts. The desire to be part of a popular T-shirt market started with Ali and Bilal during their time at university. They both wanted to be part of a dynamic business venture. However, securing funding proved to be a major challenge to these young entrepreneurs. With limited personal capital and banks showing reluctance to lend the business money, Ali and Bilal found themselves exploring options such as crowdfunding.

1 Define 'crowdfunding'.

....

....

2 Explain how Trendy Tees might use ecommerce to raise money through crowdfunding.

Think about the way the internet and mobile communications can be used to raise money.

....

....

....

....

> **TIP**
>
> This 'explain' question wants you to make the link between ecommerce and raising money for small businesses. Think about the number of potential investors the internet allows a business to reach.

3 Why do you think Trendy Tees has found it difficult to raise finance from banks and other lenders? Justify your answer.

Start your answer by explaining the problems Trendy Tees might have in raising finance from lenders. Evaluate this by setting out some of the advantages Trendy Tees might have, such as a good product in a growing market.

....

....

....

....

....

....

Activity 21.4

> **This activity focuses on sources of finance and issuing shares.**

The directors at the Canadian television production company Maple Leaf Studios have had a number of meetings to work out how they are going to tackle their $6 million cash flow problem. The company is facing a significant tax bill and many of its creditors are pushing for immediate payment. Maple Leaf's cash flow problems have been building over time, and the business has been particularly affected by the growth in online streaming, which has reduced its cash flow from revenues. Maple Leaf has also been affected by rising operating costs due to higher energy costs and rising wages. The directors are considering a new share issue worth $4 million. Some of Maple Leaf's directors are concerned about a loss of management control if new shares are issued.

1 Define 'share issue'.

   ....

   ....

2 Identify **four** types of long-term finance Maple Leaf could source funds from.

   ....

   ....

   ....

   ....

3 Explain why falling revenues and rising costs might affect Maple Leaf's cash flow.

   Think about how revenues and costs bring money in and take money out of a business such as Maple Leaf.

   ....

   ....

   ....

   ....

   ....

   ....

4   Explain **two** advantages to Maple Leaf of using share issue as a source of finance. Which advantage do you think is likely to be most important to Maple Leaf? Justify your answer.

Consider two advantages to Maple Leaf of issuing shares. Evaluate by providing a justified decision as to the biggest advantage to Maple Leaf.

....

....

....

....

....

....

....

....

REFLECTION

What have you learnt about the different types of finance businesses can use? Are you able to consider the advantages and disadvantages of different types of finance? How do you think you can improve your understanding? By practising the questions in this section and discussing your answer with others in your class, you will be able improve.

Chapter 22
Cash flow forecasts

> **LEARNING INTENTIONS**
>
> By the end of this chapter, you will be able to:
>
> - understand the importance of cash to businesses
> - understand what a cash flow forecast is and its importance
> - identify the key features of a cash flow forecast
> - amend, complete and interpret a cash flow forecast
> - understand how businesses deal with short-term cash flow problems.

> **KEY TERMS**
>
> cash flow forecast   cash inflow   cash outflow
>
> closing balance   net cash flow   opening balance

Activity 22.1

> **This activity checks your knowledge and understanding of the importance of cash flow to a business.**

Bella Pizza is a well-known UK-based pizza restaurant chain. The firm is a successful regional business that is known for its high-quality food and excellent service. However, Bella Pizza is facing challenging times in its operations due to rising costs and increasing competition. Another recent development has resulted in a significant problem for the business when one of the business's key debtors went bankrupt owing $200 000. This setback has adversely affected Bella Pizza's cash flow. The business's rising costs are also putting pressure on its cash flow.

1 Define 'net cash flow'.

   Remember to use precise terminology with 'define' questions.

   ....

   ....

2 Outline **one** source of cash inflow and **one** source of cash outflow for Bella Pizza.

   Think about the reasons why money flows into and out of the business.

   ....

   ....

3 Explain the problems to Bella Pizza's cash flow of rising costs and the failure of the debtor to pay $200 000.

Think about the impact of these events on Bella Pizza's cash inflows and outflows.

....

....

....

....

....

....

Activity 22.2

> This activity develops your skill in completing a cash flow forecast and interpreting it.

Kalila is the finance manager of Sunburst Bakery, an Algerian-based business, which is in the process of finalising the business's cash flow forecast for the coming year. With the bakery experiencing growing sales but also rising costs, effective liquidity management is important. Kalila is focused on the need for Sunburst Bakery to manage trade receivables effectively. Below is a partial cash flow forecast for Sunburst Bakery for the coming year:

$000	Jan	Feb	Mar	Apr	May	Jun
Cash inflow						
Receipts	36	36	40	42	44	46
Cash outflow						
Payments	24	44	26	36	45	48
Net cash flow	A	(8)	D	6	G	(2)
Opening balance	10	C	E	F	34	33
Closing balance	B	14	28	34	33	H

1 Define 'cash flow forecast'.

....

....

2 Calculate the missing cash flow figures in the table by filling in A–H.

Calculate the net cash flow, the opening balance and the closing balance in the table by working methodically through each month and remembering that the figures affect each other.

> **TIP**
>
> Make sure that you carefully follow the cash flow figures through the forecast in the table because one figure determines the next figure.

3 Explain the impact of rising sales and costs on Sunburst's cash flow.

Make the link between the payments needed to pay for inventory as sales rise and cash outflows.

Activity 22.3

The aim here is to further develop your skill in completing a cash flow forecast and your understanding of negative cash flow situations.

It has been a challenging year for Lumina Chile due to cash flow problems. Lumina is a Chilean-based business that manufactures and sells industrial lighting products. A downturn in sales has led to a decline in the company's liquidity position. One of the primary problems Lumina Chile faces is late payments from customers, which makes its working capital cycle difficult to manage. To deal with this, Lumina Chile is considering offering discounts to customers who agree to pay on time.

22 Cash flow forecasts

$000	Jan	Feb	Mar	Apr	May	Jun
Cash inflow						
Receipts	150	140	140	130	130	170
Cash outflow						
Payments	130	130	160	160	150	130
Net cash flow	20	10	C	E	G	40
Opening balance	10	B	D	20	(10)	(30)
Closing balance	A	40	20	F	(30)	H

1 Identify **four** sources of cash inflow.

   ....

   ....

2 Calculate the missing cash flow figures A–H in the cash flow forecast above.

   ....

   ....

   ....

   ....

3 Outline **one** way Lumina Chile might raise the funds needed to cover the negative cash flow position it faces.

   Reflect on the sources of finance from the previous unit.

   ....

   ....

   ....

4 Do you think Lumina Chile should offer discounts to customers who agree to pay on time? Justify your answer.

   Consider the advantages and disadvantages of Lumina Chile offering discounts to customers who agree to pay on time. Evaluation marks awarded for a justified decision as to whether Lumina Chile should offer discounts.

   ....

   ....

   ....

> **TIP**
>
> You need to make a judgement about the importance of liquidity to Lumina Chile in this 'justify' question. Think about the problem the business would have if it ran out of cash.

....

....

....

....

....

Activity 22.4

> **This activity gets you to consider the link between cash flow, liquidity and a significant investment.**

The management team at Indogarden, an Indonesian manufacturer of garden furniture, is planning to upgrade the company's IT system. This is a substantial investment of $560 000, and the management is carefully considering it. The company currently has a manageable liquidity position, but it is set to use $560 000 in cash to fund the project, which will place a strain on its liquidity. Indogarden has secured a $400 000 loan to part-fund the IT system investment with the remaining $160 000 coming from retained profits. The loan will, however, put pressure on future liquidity. One potential solution to ease this pressure is to delay payments to suppliers by a few days, thereby holding cash in the business for a longer period.

1   Define 'liquidity'.

....

....

2   Identify **four** ways Indogarden might use cash.

    You just need to make a list of ways here.

....

....

....

....

3 Outline **two** ways the $400 000 loan used to fund the IT investment will affect Indogarden's cash flow.

Think about the two cash outflows associated with borrowed funds.

....

....

....

....

REFLECTION

These questions require cash flow calculations. How confident do you feel in completing cash flow forecasts? Are you comfortable interpreting cash flow data? Can you think of any specific areas on this cash flow topic where you would like to improve your skills? Practicing cash flow statement questions is a useful way of improving your understanding.

Chapter 23
Statement of profit or loss

> **LEARNING INTENTIONS**
>
> By the end of this chapter, you will be able to:
>
> - understand what profit is and why it is important
> - understand the main features of a statement of profit or loss
> - make calculations based on a statement of profit or loss
> - make decisions based on a statement of profit or loss.

> **KEY TERMS**
>
> | cost of sales | expenses | gross profit | profit |
> |---|---|---|---|
> | revenue | statement of profit or loss | total cost | |

Activity 23.1

> **This activity helps to develop your understanding of revenue, costs and profits.**

Alois is the finance director at Kirschtorte, an Austrian dessert manufacturing company. He has the task of presenting to the board of directors at Kirschtorte this year's financial results. The main points of his presentation are as follows:

- 12% increase in gross profit
- 8% increase in profit
- 10% increase in total cost
- 14% increase in revenue.

1   Identify **four** types of expenses that make up Kirschtorte's total cost.

   ....

   ....

   ....

   ....

2   Outline the difference between Kirschtorte's cost of sales and expenses.

    Think about how different types of costs Kirschtorte incurs in its operations.

    ....

    ....

    ....

    ....

3   Explain **two** reasons why Kirschtorte's total costs might have increased last year.

    Think about what happens to Kirschtorte's costs when its sales increase.

    ....

    ....

    ....

    ....

    ....

    ....

    ....

4   Explain **two** advantages to Kirschtorte of having more profit. Which advantage do you think is likely to be the most important to Kirshtorte? Justify your answer.

    ....

    ....

    ....

    ....

    ....

    ....

    ....

    ....

Activity 23.2

> The aim of this activity is to test your skills in calculating profit and explaining data in a statement of profit or loss.

Techfirst is an Indian PC manufacturing company. Anil, the company's finance director, has put together the following data for Techfirst for the first half of this year. The selling price for the PCs is $200.

	Jan	Feb	Mar	Apr	May	Jun
Units sold	2700	3300	3000	2400	3000	3600
Revenue $						
Cost of sales $	324 000	396 000	360 000	288 000	360 000	432 000
Gross profit						
Expenses	108 000	108 000	108 000	108 000	108 000	108 000
Profit						

1. Outline the difference between gross profit and profit.

   Think about the different ways profit is calculated based on different types of cost.

   ....

   ....

   ....

   ....

2. Calculate Techfirst's monthly revenue for each of the first six months.

   ....

   ....

3. Calculate Techfirst's monthly gross profit for each of the first six months.

   ....

   ....

4. Calculate Techfirst's monthly profit for each of the first six months.

   Think carefully about your method in each of these calculation questions and show your working.

   ....

   ....

> **TIP**
>
> These 'calculate' questions want you to work out revenue and profit values from the data given. Remember to showing your working when you are doing this.

5   Do you think Anil will be pleased with Techfirst's financial performance over the first six months of the year? Justify your answer.

Look for areas of improvement in the data, or where financial performance has worsened.

....

....

....

....

....

....

....

Activity 23.3

This activity provides an opportunity for you to apply your understanding and make judgements about income data from different companies.

The premium shampoo market in the Danish economy is highly competitive. There are three major producers of premium shampoos: Shard, Alivio and Rinsivia. The statement of profit or loss below contains the cost, revenue and profit data for each of these producers.

$000	Shard	Alivio	Rinsivia
Revenue	245	158	187
Cost of sales	124	77	89
Gross profit			
Expenses	89	65	58
Profit			

1   Define 'revenue'.

....

....

2 Calculate the gross profit for each business.

....

....

3 Calculate the profit for each business.

....

....

4 Using appropriate ratios, which premium shampoo business do you think has performed the best? Justify your answer.

Use ratios to support your points about the performance about the different shampoo products.

....

....

....

....

....

....

....

....

Activity 23.4

> **This activity aims to develop your understanding of the relationship between profit and cash flow.**

Island Yacht Services is a successful Jamaican-based business specialising in servicing yachts. While the company's profit or loss account suggests it is experiencing rising sales and profits, it is struggling with cash flow issues. Island Yacht Services buys parts and equipment from a large supplier, which offers a short credit period. However, some of its clients, typically yacht owners, take a long time to pay their bills. Island Yacht Services's finance manager, Gabrielle, is looking for solutions to the business's cash flow problems by approaching a parts and equipment supplier who offers a longer credit period.

1 Define 'statement of profit or loss'.

....

....

2 Explain why Island Yacht Services can be profitable and in a difficult cash flow position.

Think about the difference between the times when profit and cash flow are recorded.

....

....

....

....

....

....

> **REFLECTION**
>
> Consider what you have learnt about the ways that revenue, costs and profit are recorded in the statement of profit or loss. What skills have you developed to help you to interpret profit or loss? You could discuss the questions in this chapter with your teacher to improve your understanding.

> Chapter 24

Statement of financial position

LEARNING INTENTIONS

By the end of this chapter, you will be able to:

- understand the main parts of a statement of financial position
- outline the difference between assets and liabilities
- calculate the total assets, the total liabilities and the working capital from the statement of financial position
- understand the concept of capital employed
- make decisions based on statements of financial position.

KEY TERMS

assets   capital employed   current assets   current liabilities

liabilities   non-current assets   non-current liabilities

owner's or shareholders' equity   statement of financial position

trade payables   trade receivables

Activity 24.1

This activity checks your understanding of the basic make-up of the statement of financial position.

Harmony Hub is a chain of musical instrument shops planning to acquire another music store called Melody Hill. The financial director at Harmony Hub has been analysing Melody Hill's statement of financial position to determine whether to go ahead with the purchase. The statement of financial position values Melody Hill's non-current assets are valued at $1.5 million.

1   Define 'non-current assets'.

   Remember to use precise terminology with this 'definition' question.

   ....

   ....

2 Identify **four** types of Melody Hill's non-current assets.

You just need to make a list here.

....

....

....

....

Activity 24.2

In this activity, you are expected to show your knowledge of the different items in the statement of financial position.

Table 24.1 sets out examples of the following items in the statement of financial position for a car dealership:

- non-current asset
- current asset
- current liability
- non-current liability
- owner's or shareholders' equity.

Match each of the examples with the different items in the statement of financial position.

Table 24.1: Different items in the statement of financial position

Example	Statement item
Retained profits	
Shares issued by the business	
New cars on sales	
Car showroom	
Money owed to the business by its customers	
The business's bank overdraft	
Money owed by the business to its suppliers	
Cash in the bank	
Shares issued by the business	
Inventory of car parts and accessories	

> **TIP**
>
> Remember how the figures in the statement of financial position are related to each other when you are answering numerical questions on this topic.

Activity 24.3

> The aim of this activity is to develop your understanding of the different components in the statement of financial position.

Zam Beverage is a Zambian soft drinks manufacturer that has had a successful year and has increased its market share. Sales revenue has increased by nearly 40% over the past two years, leading to a 25% rise in retained profits. However, this growth in sales has resulted in a significant increase in the inventories that Zam Beverage needs to maintain their business. The company's statement of financial position is given below.

	$000
Non-current assets	700
Current assets	400
Less:	
Current liabilities	290
Net current assets	A
Net assets	B
Financed by:	
Owner's equity	C
Non-current liabilities	290
Capital employed	D

1 Outline the difference between non-current assets and current assets.

   ....

   ....

   ....

   ....

2 Calculate Zam Beverage's statement of financial position by completing the missing figures A–D.

   Focus on how the figures in the statement of financial position are related to one another.

   ....

   ....

   ....

   ....

3 Explain how Zam Beverage's capital employed is affected by the increase in the value of its buildings.

You need to make the connection between capital employed and net assets here.

....

....

....

....

....

....

> **TIP**
>
> 'Explain' questions are looking for you to make links to show how and why things happen.

Activity 24.4

The questions in this activity develop your understanding of how the statement of financial position is important to stakeholders.

Shoei Co is a public limited company, a leading Japanese footwear manufacturer, that produces a wide range of footwear from boots and training shoes to formal shoes. The company is looking to borrow an additional $50 million from a major commercial bank to finance its growth plans. The bank has expressed concerns about the company's existing borrowing and the additional interest payments it will incur with the new loan. Shoei Co's statement of financial position is set out below.

	$000	$000
Non-current assets		
Property	280 000	
Machinery	120 000	
Equipment	85 000	
Total		A
Current assets		
Inventories	46 000	
Trade receivables	58 000	
Cash	27 000	
Total		131 000

	$000	$000
Current liabilities		
Overdraft	B	
Trade payables	38 000	
Short-term loan	25 000	
Total		107 000
Net current asset		24 000
Net asset		509 000
Equity		
Share capital	280 000	
Retained profits	130 000	
Total		**C**
Long-term liabilities		99 000
Capital employed		**D**

1 Define 'owner's equity'.

....

....

2 Calculate the missing figures for A–D in Shoei Co's statement of financial position.

Be careful to show the relationship between the different figures in the statement of financial position.

....

....

....

....

....

....

3   Explain the effect the proposed $50 million loan would have on Shoei Co's statement of financial position.

    Try to make the link between changes in the value of borrowing and capital employed.

    ....

    ....

    ....

    ....

    ### REFLECTION

    How confident are you about making connections between a statement of financial position and the performance of a business? What skills do you feel you could improve to make your understanding clearer? Complete the questions in this chapter and discuss your answers with someone else in your class to improve your understanding.

Chapter 25
Analysis of accounts

LEARNING INTENTIONS

By the end of this chapter, you will be able to:

- understand the concept of profitability
- understand the concept of liquidity
- calculate profitability ratios and liquidity ratios
- explain how stakeholders might use financial information to help make decisions
- outline the limitations of using accounts and ratio analysis.

KEY TERM

liquidity

Activity 25.1

This activity develops your understanding of the basic principles of measuring business performance using ratio analysis.

Green Haven is a successful garden centre in New Zealand specialising in a wide variety of plants, gardening tools and landscaping services. However, the company is currently experiencing difficulties, and several important stakeholders are concerned about the business's prospects. The emergence of new competition in the market has started to put pressure on Green Haven's profit margins. Below is the financial data for Green Haven for three years presented in Table 25.1:

Table 25.1: Revenue, profit and equity figure for Green Haven

$000	2021	2022	2023
Revenue	3200	3150	3120
Profit	310	290	260
Total equity	2450	2560	2610

1 Define 'profit margin'.

   Be precise and accurate with this 'definition' question.

   ....

   ....

25 Analysis of accounts

2 Explain why Green Haven's total equity might have increased from 2021 to 2023.

   You need to think about the link between Green Haven's retained profits and total equity.

   ....

   ....

   ....

   ....

   ....

   ....

> **TIP**
>
> This 'explain' question is asking you to set out the link between equity and profit. To be analytical, you need to show clear reasoning between these two factors.

3 Calculate Green Haven's profit margins for 2021–2023.

   Remember to show your working with these calculations.

   ....

   ....

   ....

   ....

   ....

   ....

4 Explain **two** possible reasons for the change in Green Haven's profit margins from 2021 to 2023.

   Think about the impact revenues and costs can have on a business's profit margin.

   ....

   ....

   ....

....

....

....

Activity 25.2

This set of questions will help you check your understanding of, and the ability to apply, the ratios for gross profit margin, profit margin and return on capital employed.

Klima Plus and Cool Croatia are two of the top manufacturers of air conditioning units in Croatia. Both companies are performing well in a rapidly growing market. The total market sales for air conditioning units in Croatia has risen by 18% annually for the past two years. Both companies are now looking to raise additional finance, and potential investors are keen to evaluate their financial performance. Below is the financial data for Klima Plus and Cool Croatia presented in Table 25.2:

Table 25.2: Revenue, profit and capital employed figures for Klima Plus and Cool Croatia

$m	Klima Plus	Cool Croatia
Revenue	22	15
Gross profit	12	8
Expenses	7	5
Profit	5	3
Capital employed	12	11

1   Outline the difference between gross profit margin and profit margin.

....

....

....

....

25 Analysis of accounts

2 Using the data in Table 25.2, calculate gross profit margin, profit margin and return on capital employed for Klima Plus and Cool Croatia.

Make sure that you show your working in this calculation question.

....

....

....

....

....

....

3 Explain which business has performed the best in terms of gross profit margin, profit margin and return on capital employed.

You need to think about the link between the revenue each business generates and how much gross profit and profit each business earns.

....

....

....

....

....

....

4 Do you think the advantages to Klima Plus and Cool Croatia of using return on capital employed to measure performance are greater than the disadvantages? Justify your answer.

Think about the reasons why it is advantageous for Klima Plus and Cool Croatia to use ROCE to measure performance. Can you think of any potential disadvantages?

....

....

....

BUSINESS FOR CAMBRIDGE IGCSE™ AND O LEVEL: WORKBOOK

....

....

....

....

....

Activity 25.3

This activity focuses on the use of ratios to measure a business's liquidity.

Things are difficult at Sound Mist, a Portuguese speaker manufacturer. The company is in the middle of a significant liquidity crisis because of poor economic conditions. Sound Mist's speaker sales are falling because of pressure on household incomes and new competition in the market. The business's cash flow problems got worse when one of its biggest customers went bankrupt and many of its debtors are taking longer to pay. Current assets, current liabilities and inventory figures for Sound Mist are shown in Table 25.3.

Table 25.3: Current assets, current liabilities and inventory figures for Sound Mist

$000	2022	2023
Current assets	43	52
Inventories	28	35
Current liabilities	23	32

1   State the equations for the current ratio and the acid test ratio.

    You just need to write out the equations here.

    ....

    ....

2   Calculate the current ratio and the acid test ratio for Sound Mist for 2022 and 2023.

    ....

    ....

    ....

    ....

3   Explain what Sound Mist's current ratio and acid test ratio values say about the business's liquidity.

Make the link between values of the current and acid test ratios and the ease with which Sound Mist can access cash.

....

....

....

....

Activity 25.4

The aim of this activity is to use ratio analysis on the statement of financial position and statement of profit or loss to judge a business's performance.

Solar VT sells solar panels and its components. It has been a good year for the business, a market leader in Tanzania's renewable energy market, with a significant rise in its ROCE. The renewable energy market is growing and the business's market share is increasing. Solar VT is known for its high-quality products and excellent customer service. The business has recently invested $13 million in a new manufacturing plant and is funding this investment through a combination of a new share issue and retained profits. Below is Solar VT's statement of financial position, followed by its statement of profit or loss.

Statement of financial position		
$m	2022	2023
Non-current assets	43	51
Current assets	18	20
Less:		
Current liabilities	11	13
Net current assets	7	7
Net assets	50	58
Financed by:		
Owner's equity	42	50
Non-current liabilities	8	8
Capital employed	50	58

Statement of profit or loss		
$m	2022	2023
Revenue	22	28
Cost of sales	14	18
Gross profit	8	10
Expenses	3	4
Profit	5	6

1. Define 'return on capital employed'.

   ....

   ....

2. Using Solar VT's statement of profit or loss and statement of financial position, calculate the following ratios for 2022 and 2023:

   - gross profit margin
   - profit margin
   - return on capital employed.

   ....

   ....

   ....

   ....

   ....

   ....

TIP

When you are working on this calculation question, make sure you lay out your numerical answer clearly and always show your working.

3. Using Solar VT's statement of financial position, calculate the current ratio for 2022 and 2023 and outline what the change in its value says about the business's liquidity.

   Describe the change in Solar VT's liquidity based on your ratio calculation.

   ....

   ....

   ....

   ....

4 Explain what Solar VT's profit margin and return on capital employed say about the business's performance from 2022 to 2023.

Try to think about the links between revenues, profits and the value of Solar VT's long-term finance.

....

....

....

....

....

....

REFLECTION

What have you learnt about the relationship between the data in a business's statement of profit or loss and statement of financial position? Are there ways you could improve your understanding of these two statements?

Section 5 Practice questions

Practice question 1

Peg-it manufactures high-quality tents. Its Finance Director knows that profit is important and has set an objective of increasing Peg-it's profits by 5% in the next five years. She is thinking about increasing price or switching to a cheaper supplier to increase its gross profit. Table 1 shows a summary of Peg-it's statement of profit or loss. There are internal and external users of accounts who use this information to make decisions.

Table 1: Summary of Peg-it's statement of profit or loss

	Statement of profit or loss	
$000	**2024**	**2025**
Revenue	1 200	1 250
Cost of sales	640	625
Gross profit	560	625
Expenses	350	360
Profit	210	265

a   Calculate Peg-it's gross profit margin in 2025. [2]

b   Identify **four** reasons why profit is important to a business. [4]

c   Explain how **one** internal user and **one** external user could use Peg-it's accounts to make decisions. [6]

d   Do you think Peg-it should increase price or switch to a cheaper supplier to increase its gross profit? Justify your answer. [8]

Total available marks: 20

> **WORKED EXAMPLE**
>
> ### Question 1c
>
> Internal user: Shareholders [K]. They will be interested to see if they are going to get a good return on their investment [An] into the tent manufacturer [Ap].
>
> External user: Suppliers [K]. They will be interested to see if the business is likely to be able to pay for materials on time [An], particularly as the cost of sales is forecast to increase to $625 000 [Ap].

Section 5 Practice questions

Improve this answer

This is a sample answer to Practice question 1d. The answer contains some weaknesses. Read through this answer and consider how it could be improved.

Increase price: If Peg-it increases price then it may experience a decrease in demand [K]. This could lead to a loss of revenue [An].

Decrease cost of sales: Switching to a cheaper supplier may decrease the quality of materials [K] used by the tent manufacturer [Ap].

Justification: I think that increasing price is the best way to improve gross profit. Customers may be prepared to pay a higher price for a good quality product, so sales and revenue may not fall by very much [E].

Your challenge

See whether you can improve this answer. This answer has many positives. There is a relevant impact of an increase in price identified, with development of the impact of this. However, there is no reference to the case study for this point. The point about switching to a cheaper supplier is valid, and there is reference to the case study. However, there is no development of this point to explain the impact. There is a partial judgement provided, however, this needs to be developed further to cover the evaluation part of this question.

CASE STUDY 1

NKFC is a football team based in Country X. It is a private limited company. Attendance at its football matches has been increasing for the last three years. Customers can pay for tickets in full when they purchase the ticket, or can spread the cost of their ticket over a three-month period. NKFC has a team bus that takes the players to fixtures that are not played at its home ground. The bus is 14 years old.

The Finance Director has produced a cash flow forecast. A summary of the cash flow forecast is shown in Appendix 1. He is worried about the negative cash flow in March 2025 and is thinking about using an overdraft or asking customers to pay more quickly to overcome this cash flow problem.

Some stakeholders are concerned about the profitability of NKFC. Appendix 2 shows a summary of NKFC's profit and loss data for the last two years.

NKFC is thinking about its liquidity. A summary of its Statement of Financial Position is shown in Appendix 3.

NKFC is considering upgrading the stadium to increase its capacity. It is thinking about different sources of finance that could be used to fund the investment. Sources of finance that could be used include a bank loan and issuing of shares. The Finance Director knows there are many others reasons why finance is important.

Appendix 1

Summary of NKFC's Cash flow forecast 2025

$000	January	February	March
Cash inflow			
Receipts	77	82	80
Cash outflow			
Payments	A	78	85
Net cash flow	(4)	C	(5)
Opening balance	2	(2)	D
Closing balance	B	2	(3)

Appendix 2

Summary of NKFC's Statement of profit or loss for 2024 and 2025

$000	2024	2025
Revenue	950	920
Cost of sales	444	368
Gross profit	506	552
Expenses	321	368
Profit	185	184

Appendix 3

Summary of NKFC's Statement of financial position for 2024 and 2025

Statement of financial position		
$000	2024	2025
Non-current assets	1532	1584
Current assets	246	275
Cash	160	150
Inventory	86	125
Less:		
Current liabilities	123	125
Net current assets	123	150

Section 5 Practice questions

1 a Explain **two** reasons why finance is important to NKFC.

Reason 1:

Explanation:

Reason 2:

Explanation: [8]

b Use Appendix 3 and other information to consider NKFC's liquidity position. Do you think NKFC's liquidity position has improved from 2024 to 2025? Justify your answer.

NKFC's liquidity position:

Conclusion: [12]

2 a Explain **two** reasons why profit is important to NKFC.

Reason 1:

Explanation:

Reason 2:

Explanation: [8]

b Consider the following **two** sources of finance that NKFC are thinking about using for the expansion of the stadium. Which source do you think NKFC should use? Justify your answer.

Share issue:

Bank loan:

Conclusion: [12]

3 a i Calculate the values for A, B, C and D in NKFC's cash flow forecast (Appendix 1).

A:

B:

C:

D:

ii Identify **four** reasons why cash is important to a business.

Reason 1:

Reason 2:

Reason 3:

Reason 4: [8]

b Consider the advantages and disadvantages of the following **two** methods NKFC could use to solve its short-term cash flow problem. Which method do you think NKFC should use? Justify your answer.

Overdraft:

Asking customers to pay more quickly:

Conclusion: [12]

4 a i Using Appendix 2, calculate NKFC's gross profit margin for 2025.

   ii Using Appendix 2, calculate NKFC's profit margin for 2025.

   iii Identify **four** stakeholders that might be interested in the accounts of a business. [8]

b Use Appendix 2 and other information to consider NKFC's profitability. Do you think NKFC's profitability has improved from 2024 to 2025? Justify your answer.

NKFC's profitability:

Conclusion: [12]

Total available marks: 80

WORKED EXAMPLE

Question 2a

Reason 1: It can act as a source of finance [**K**].

Explanation: NKFC is looking to expand its stadium [**Ap**] so profit could be used for this. This can reduce the need for borrowing from other sources [**An**], which can reduce costs [**An**].

Reason 2: It acts as a reward for risk-taking [**K**].

Explanation: NKFC is a private limited company [**Ap**]. Profits may attract new investors into the business [**An**], this can increase the amount of funds available for investment [**An**].

Improve this answer

This is a sample answer to Practice question 2b. Read through this answer and consider how it could be improved.

Share issue: Share issue is beneficial as it is a form of permanent capital [K]. However, having more shareholders dilutes the ownership of the original owners [K].

Bank loan: Large sums of money can be borrowed [K]. This means that NKFC are likely to be able to borrow to amount needed to fund the expansion of the stadium [Ap]. However, interest must be paid on a bank loan [K].

Conclusion: I think that a bank loan is the best method. Even though the break-even point will increase, they will be able to sell more tickets due to the increased capacity therefore it should not be difficult to achieve this new break-even point. Shareholders could be unhappy if dividends are not paid and could withdraw their investment, meaning another source is required to be used [**E**].

Your challenge

See whether you can improve this answer.

There is some good knowledge demonstrated throughout with advantages and disadvantages of both sources of finance given. However, there is no real development of any point. Try to develop each of the advantages and disadvantages into chains of analysis. Use the judgement to help you think about what the analysis could be. This is a justified decision made in context.

# Section 6
External influences on business activity

> Chapter 26
Economic issues

> **LEARNING INTENTIONS**
>
> By the end of this chapter, you will be able to:
>
> - explain the main stages of the business cycle and how each stage of the business cycle might affect a business
> - describe the effects of changes in the levels of employment, inflation and economic growth on a business
> - describe the effects of government policy – changes in government spending and interest rates as well as taxes – on business profit and people's income
> - understand how businesses respond to changes in taxes and interest rates.

> **KEY TERMS**
>
> economic growth   inflation   interest rate
>
> level of unemployment   tax

Activity 26.1

> This activity will help you demonstrate your understanding of the different stages of the business cycle and the impact it has on individuals and businesses.

Jomo Tractors is a public limited company that produces tractors in Kenya. Jomo Tractors has always been profitable since it was set up 30 years ago.

In the third quarter of 2020, Kenya slid into a recession for the first time in at least two decades as the impact of the COVID-19 pandemic continued to hurt output. But, as of 2023, Kenya's gross domestic product (GDP) has been increasing and the economy is growing. Unemployment is falling and the government is reviewing its policies to stimulate further growth. However, inflation is starting to increase and become a problem.

1   Identify and explain **two** characteristics of recession.

    Look at the key characteristics of the economy.

    ....

    ....

    ....

    ....

2 State which stage of the business cycle Kenya's economy is in during 2023.

Link the economic indicators to what the economic objectives might be.

....

....

3 Explain the effect of increasing inflation on individuals and businesses such as Jomo Tractors.

....

....

....

....

4 Explain why a low level of unemployment may be important objective for the Government of Kenya.

....

....

....

....

5 Explain the advantages and disadvantages of falling unemployment on businesses such as Jomo Tractors.

....

....

....

....

....

....

Activity 26.2

> In this activity, you will use your knowledge and understanding of how a government controls its main sources of income to analyse its impact on consumers and businesses.

With the economy of the country in the growth stage, the Government of India wants to increase its income so that it can spend more on its infrastructure and public services. It has reviewed its policies and has increased its business taxes but has decreased its tax on people's income.

1   State **two** main sources of a government's income.

    ....

    ....

2   Explain how increased government spending on infrastructure will be beneficial for the people and businesses in India.

    ....

    ....

    ....

    ....

Figure 26.1 shows the business tax rate in India from 2019 to 2023.

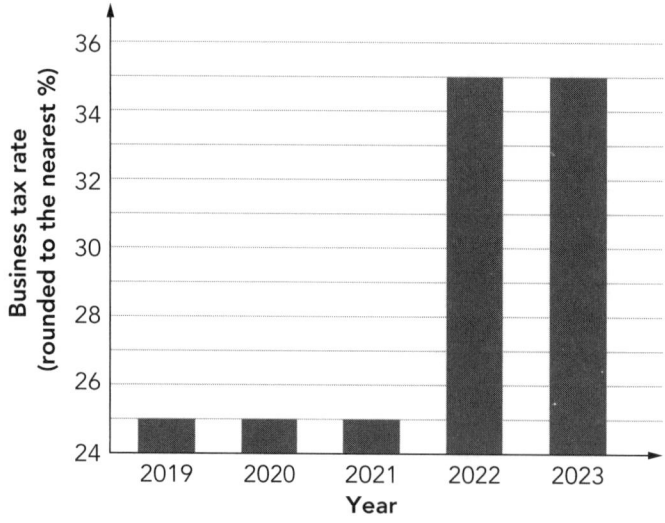

Figure 26.1: Business tax rate in India, 2019–2023

3 Outline the change in the business tax rate over the past five years.

First, analyse the graph and identify the change/trend. What was the lowest and highest tax rate in the five-year time period? Support this with data from Figure 26.1.

....

....

4 Identify **two** effects of the changes in the business tax rate on the businesses in India.

....

....

....

....

5 Explain the effect of a decrease in people's income tax rate on consumers and businesses in India.

....

....

....

....

Activity 26.3

In this activity, you will be using your knowledge and understanding of how governments control the amount of money in circulation by changing interest rates.

XYZ Solar is a public limited company based in Texas, USA. It manufactures solar panels and is thinking of expanding its operations into neighbouring Mexico, where there is a growing market for green energy such as solar energy. To fund this expansion, XYZ Solar's finance manager is planning on taking a loan. He is worried about the rising interest rates from 2021 to 2024 (see Table 26.1). He has also noticed that inflation steadily decreased in 2023 before rising again in 2024 (see Figure 26.2).

Table 26.1: Interest rates in the last five years up to 2024

Year	Interest rate (%)
2020	2.8
2021	0.2
2022	0.2
2023	4.5
2024	5.5

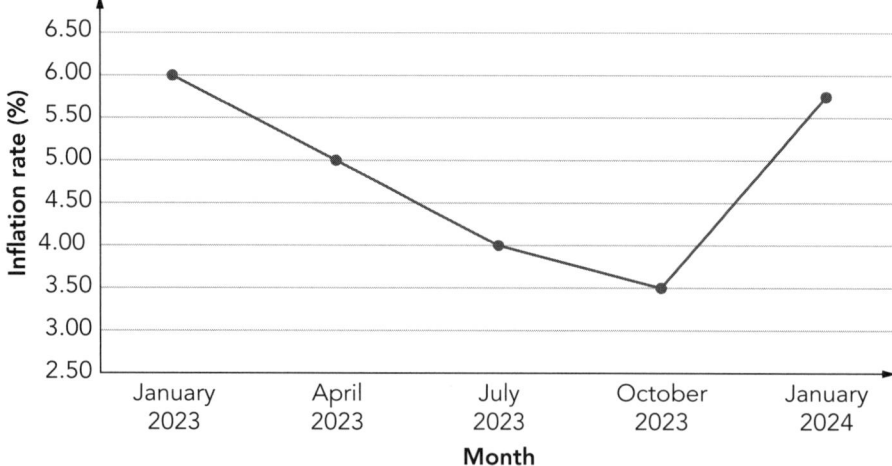

Figure 26.2: Inflation in 2023–2024

XYZ Solar's finance manager is worried about the impact of increasing interest rates on the costs.

1   Define 'interest rate'.

    ....

    ....

2   Calculate the amount of interest that will have to be paid in the year 2020 on a loan amount of $2 000 000.

    ....

    ....

3 Outline how the interest rates have changed from 2020 to 2024. How might the change in interest rates have affected XYZ Solar's profits and expansion plans?

....

....

....

....

4 Explain how the change in interest rates from 2022 to 2024 may have affected consumer spending on XYZ Solar's products.

....

....

> **TIP**
>
> When a question includes data, whether it is in a chart/graph or a table, always put it in context by reading the title and the column headings. If the data is given for a number of years, then look at the trend (upward or downward shift) over time.

5 Explain the impact of increasing inflation on XYZ Solar's sales.

Try to answer the question in context by using information from the question.

....

....

....

....

6 Do you think that the finance manager of XYZ Solar should be worried about the increasing interest rates? Justify your answer.

Remember to use information from the context as the question refers specifically to XYZ Solar.

....

....

....

....

....

....

....

> **TIP**
>
> When justifying your opinion on a business decision, always consider the points in favour of and against the decision. Give the reasons for your viewpoint and explain why you support it. To make your viewpoint more convincing, explain the disadvantages of the opposite point of view as well.

> **REFLECTION**
>
> Think about the various aspects of government policy and how changing them affects people and businesses. Which factors can you describe the best and which do you find more difficult? Why were they difficult? Was it a gap in your knowledge and understanding or did you find it hard to apply your knowledge to answer the activities? How can you improve your understanding? What skills do you think were useful in answering the data-based questions? Do you feel confident working with percentages and reading graphs and tables?

> Chapter 27
Business and the international economy

LEARNING INTENTIONS

By the end of this chapter, you will be able to:

- understand the reasons for globalisation and its opportunities and threats for businesses
- discuss import tariffs and import quotas and their effects on businesses
- understand what a multinational company (MNC) is and the advantages to a business of becoming an MNC
- discuss the advantages and disadvantages for a country where a multinational company is located
- understand and analyse the external costs and external benefits of business decisions
- explain the impact of appreciation and depreciation of exchange rates on importers and exporters of products and services.

KEY TERMS

appreciation   depreciation   exchange rate   external benefit
external cost   globalisation   import quota
import tariff   multinational company (MNC)

Activity 27.1

This activity checks your knowledge and understanding of key concepts, and also requires you to analyse the impact of multinational companies and apply this to the given scenario.

Seka Automobiles (SA) is a successful automobile manufacturer based in Germany. It exports its cars and trucks to various countries in the region. It is looking forward to launching its first hybrid vehicle (one that works on petrol as well as electricity) soon. With increased demand of hybrid vehicles and the continued growth in globalisation in recent years, the senior executives of the company think that the company should take advantage of it and are considering setting up a manufacturing plant in Singapore and becoming a multinational company.

1. Define 'globalisation'.

   ....

   ....

2. Identify and explain **two** reasons for the growth of globalisation.

   ....

   ....

   ....

   ....

3. Define 'multinational company'.

   ....

   ....

4. Explain **two** reasons why SA may want to become a multinational company.

   Start by identifying and explaining two advantages of becoming a multinational company. Then, explain the effect of these advantages on SA and try to use some of the information given in the question.

   ....

   ....

   ....

   ....

   ....

   ....

Activity 27.2

> This activity checks your understanding of the factors to be considered by companies when doing business internationally.

Yoko Toys (YT) manufactures electronic toys and video games in its factory in Philippines. It started exporting its products to its neighbouring countries, including Malaysia and Indonesia, five years ago. In the last year, however, Malaysia introduced import tariffs and import quotas. Both Malaysia and Indonesia, have a good potential market and YT's exports have been increasing to these countries every year.

YT is evaluating whether becoming a multinational company and setting up operations in Malaysia and Indonesia may be a more profitable option than just exporting there. It does not have the capital to set up operations in both countries and so must choose one.

1 Define 'import tariff'.

   ....

   ....

2 Define 'import quota'.

   ....

   ....

3 Outline the possible effects of import tariffs and import quotas on YT.

   ....

   ....

   ....

   ....

4 Explain **two** factors that YT should consider before setting up its operations in Malaysia.

   ....

   ....

   ....

   ....

Activity 27.3

> This activity relies on your understanding of exchange rates. The last question tests your ability to analyse the impact of exchange rate changes on importers and exporters and your ability to develop a link to the impact on consumers.

ABC Electronics is a public limited company that produces electronic equipment in China. It imports some of the components and raw materials needed for manufacturing electronic equipment from the United States. It also exports its products to the United States. The exchange rate between China's currency, the Yuan (CNY), and the United States's currency, the US dollar (USD), is:

USD:CNY is 1:7

Over a period of time, the value of China's currency appreciates against the value of the United States's currency.

1 Explain 'exchange rate'.

   ....

   ....

2 Calculate the value of $20 000 in Yuan.

   ....

   ....

   ....

   ....

TIP

When working out amounts in different currencies, use your knowledge of ratios to use the given exchange rate.

3 Define 'appreciation'.

   Remember that appreciation should be considered with respect to another currency appreciation, in this case, the USD.

   ....

   ....

4 Explain the effect of the appreciation of the CNY against the USD on the imports that ABC Electronics makes for manufacturing the electronic equipment.

....

....

....

....

5 Explain the effect of the appreciation of the CNY against the USD on the exports of ABC Electronics and its consumers in the United States.

First, identify the main impact of appreciation of the CNY on the price of ABC Electronics's products. Then, explain what impact this will have on the consumers. This can then be developed further to explain how the customers will react and in turn what its impact will be on ABC Electronics.

....

....

....

....

....

....

REFLECTION

How well can you explain the impact of the appreciation and depreciation of exchange rates on businesses, both import and export? Can you think of any ways to help you remember this? Have you tried using visual aids such as mind maps or diagrams?

Chapter 28
Environmental and ethical issues

> **LEARNING INTENTIONS**
>
> By the end of this chapter, you will be able to:
>
> - discuss how business activity can negatively affect the environment
> - understand how and why businesses might respond to environmental issues
> - outline the effects of legal controls over business activity affecting the environment
> - understand the ethical issues that might affect businesses
> - understand how businesses respond to ethical issues and the advantages and disadvantages of being ethical
> - understand the role of pressure groups and how they can influence business decisions.

> **KEY TERM**
>
> pressure group

Activity 28.1

This activity will check your understanding of the environmental impact of business activity and why and how businesses respond.

Cyclo Plastics (CP) plans to set up a new manufacturing plant near a major city in India. It plans to manufacture household items made of recycled plastic. It has presented its proposal but is waiting for the government's approval. The government has recently introduced incentives to encourage businesses to be more environmentally friendly. Stricter environmental regulations and legal controls have also been introduced to reduce pollution. In its proposal, CP has included a plan for proper waste disposal from its factory along with other steps that it will take to reduce the negative effects on the environment.

1   Identify **two** types of pollution.

    ....

    ....

2   Identify **two** steps that CP is taking to be an environmentally friendly business.

    ....

    ....

3 Identify and explain **two** legal controls that Government of India can use to discourage the negative impact of businesses on the environment.

....

....

....

....

4 Discuss **two** ways businesses such as CP can reduce their negative impact on the environment.

....

....

....

....

....

5 Explain **two** reasons why CP might respond to environmental issues. Which reason do you think is the most important to CP? Justify your answer.

Think about the reasons why CP might respond to environmental issues. How might CP be affected if they did not respond?

....

....

....

....

....

> **TIP**
>
> In questions requiring the skills of analysis, application and evaluation, choosing the right knowledge points/factors to develop further is very important. Choose the knowledge points that can be analysed in detail, support multiple points of view and relate well to the business in context.

Activity 28.2

> In this activity, you will have to use your knowledge and understanding of how pressure groups work and how businesses respond to environmental pressures.

Yummy Foods (YF) is an international fast-food chain serving food from all over the world. It wants to expand by starting operations in country Y, which has specific cultural and religious practices. YF hopes to benefit from the low cost of labour and gain access to more consumers.

However, there has been a lot of negative press about this venture in country Y and pressure groups are filing a petition to oppose this. They are holding demonstrations saying that this will have a negative impact environmentally, economically and culturally. They claim that the fast food sold by YF will be harmful for health and will interfere with the cultural and religious practices of country Y. They also claim that the high amounts of packaging and waste produced by disposable ware will be bad for the environment and that the local restaurants and cafes will be affected negatively. The pressure groups are lobbying to persuade the government to revisit its legal controls.

1. Define 'pressure group'.

2. Explain **three** methods used by the pressure groups to make their point.

3. Identify and explain **one** negative impact on the local restaurants and cafes.

TIP

When evaluating a business decision, consider both sides of the decision and always develop the knowledge points/factors and analyse them fully instead of listing various factors. Analyse the factors for their impact and link this back to the question. To come to a well-justified evaluation, explain the greater significance of one side of the argument over the other.

28 Environmental and ethical issues

4 Explain why it is important for YF to respond to the threats and opportunities provided by the pressure groups.

   Remember to answer the question in context as YF has not started operations yet.

   ....

   ....

   ....

   ....

5 As highlighted by the pressure group, identify the **four** effects of YF opening outlets in country Y. Which **two** effects do you think are the most significant?

   Read the information in the question carefully to identify the claims made by the pressure groups about YF and explain the impact on country Y.

   ....

   ....

   ....

   ....

   ....

6 Explain **two** legal controls over business activity affecting the environment that may impact YF. Which legal control do you think is likely to have the biggest effect for YF? Justify your answer.

   Think about different legal controls affecting the environment that may impact YF. Evaluate by making a justified decision as to which one is likely to be the most important to YF.

   ....

   ....

   ....

   ....

....

....

....

....

Activity 28.3

> This activity relies on your understanding of ethical issues faced by businesses and the conflict that they have between profits and ethics when making business decisions.

Nature's Glow (NG) manufactures organic skin care products and sells its products in the international market. It has been facing a lot of opposition from an international pressure group due to its suspected unethical business practices. The pressure group claims that:

- NG is violating the basic labour rights on pay and health and safety in the workplace.
- NG products do not meet the strict regulatory standards of the cosmetic industry in terms of sourcing ingredients ethically and thoroughly testing products for human safety.

NG denies the claims, but due to increasing pressure from its stakeholders, it set up a committee to investigate the claims made by the pressure group.

The initial findings of the inquiry have found that NG's main supplier, who is in a different country, has had a lot of negative press in the local media about its unethical business practices. Even though, NG has always worked with this supplier and gets many trade discounts from them, it is wondering if it should find an alternative supplier.

Additionally, there was an article in the media about the latest regulatory standards in the cosmetic industry and concerns over NG products not meeting the strict testing standards.

1 What is an unethical business decision?

....

....

28 Environmental and ethical issues

2 Identify and explain **two** unethical business practices of NG towards its workers.

Read the information in the question carefully to identify the claims made by the pressure groups about NG's unethical business practices and explain the impact on the workers.

....

....

....

....

....

3 Explain how the unethical business practices by its suppliers might affect NG's consumers in the market.

....

....

....

....

....

4 Identify and explain **one** advantage and **one** disadvantage to NG of making its business practices more ethical.

....

....

....

....

....

....

REFLECTION

What is challenging about evaluating the ethical impact of business decisions? Did you analyse the factors from just the perspective of a business or from other stakeholders too? What skills do you think were useful? How could you develop these skills further?

Section 6 Practice questions

Practice question 1

EcoTextiles is a multinational company that sells environmentally friendly clothes. Its target market is women. It manufactures its clothes in a factory in Country X and distributes them all around the world. EcoTextiles has 700 employees. One of the main objectives of EcoTextiles is to respond to environmental issues. It is also focused on being ethical.

a Define 'multinational company'. [2]

b Outline **two** advantages to EcoTextiles of being a multinational company. [4]

c Explain **two** advantages to EcoTextiles of being ethical. [6]

d Explain **two** reasons why EcoTextiles may respond to environmental issues. Which reason is likely to be the most important to EcoTextiles? Justify your answer. [8]

Total available marks: 20

WORKED EXAMPLE

Question 1d

Reason 1: Improved reputation [**K**]. This could lead to more choice of potential employees for the business [**An**] if they need to employ more than, or replace any of, the 700 workers [**Ap**].

Reason 2: Increase sales [**K**] for the clothing manufacturer [**Ap**]. This leads to an increase in revenue [**An**].

Justification: I think that improved reputation is the most important reason. This provides a range of advantages such as more choice of potential employees or more likely to attract investors, as well as increasing sales. While the reason of increasing sales is important, this could naturally happen if EcoTextiles has a strong reputation [**E**].

Improve this answer

This is a sample answer to Practice question 1c. The answer contains some weaknesses. Read through this answer and consider how it could be improved.

Advantage 1: Better brand image [K]. This can lead to an increase in sales [An].

Advantage 2: Able to charge higher prices [K] when selling to women [Ap].

Your challenge

See whether you can improve this answer. Advantage 1 is valid and has been developed into a relevant chain of analysis. However, there is no link to the business context. Advantage 2 is also valid and shows good application, however there is no development of the knowledge point therefore no analysis has been given for this advantage.

> ### CASE STUDY 1
>
> **Mejor Cafe**
>
> Mejor Cafe sells drinks, including coffee, in Country X. Its sales and profits have increased for the last five years. One of Mejor Cafe's main objectives is to be an ethical business. It pairs fair wages to its employees and uses suppliers that do not damage the environment. This means that pressure groups do not try to influence the decisions of Mejor Cafe.
>
> Mejor Cafe's contract with its coffee bean supplier ends this year. It will need to find a new supplier when the contract runs out. Many suppliers are based in other countries, which means that changes in the exchange rate could affect Mejor Cafe. This could affect their costs and price the cafe charges for its drinks. Economic growth has increased in Country X, and unemployment has fallen.
>
> The government has increased tax on people's income in Country X. This will reduce the amount of income that consumers have, and could also mean that employees are less motivated than before. The Managing Director is thinking about how these effects could affect Mejor Cafe. The government is also thinking about increasing tax on business profit. This could affect shareholders dividends and the funds Mejor Cafe has available to reinvest. The tax revenue will be used to increase government spending.
>
> The central bank in Country X is thinking about decreasing interest rates. Mejor Cafe could benefit from this decrease in many different ways.

1 a Explain **one** advantage and **one** disadvantage to Mejor Cafe of Country X experiencing economic growth.

   Advantage:

   Explanation:

   Disadvantage:

   Explanation: [8]

 b Consider the following **two** effects of an increase in taxes on people's income. Which effect is likely to have the biggest impact on Mejor Cafe? Justify your answer.

   Consumers have less income:

   Employees might not be as motivated:

   Conclusion: [12]

2 a Explain **two** advantages to Mejor Cafe of a decrease in interest rates.

   Advantage 1:

   Explanation:

   Advantage 2:

   Explanation: [8]

 b Consider the advantages and disadvantages of the following **two** ways in which Mejor Cafe is being ethical. Which way is likely to be the most important for Mejor Cafe? Justify your answer.

   Paying fair wages to employees:

   Using suppliers that do not damage the environment:

   Conclusion: [12]

3 a Explain **one** advantage and **one** disadvantage to Mejor Cafe of a decrease in unemployment in Country X.

   Advantage:

   Explanation:

   Disadvantage:

   Explanation: [8]

 b Consider how an appreciation in the exchange rate could affect Mejor Cafe in the following **two** ways. Which way do you think is the most important for Mejor Cafe? Justify your answer.

   Costs:

   Price:

   Conclusion: [12]

Section 6 Practice questions

4 a Explain **two** ways pressure groups could influence Mejor Cafe's decisions.

Way 1:

Explanation:

Way 2:

Explanation: [8]

b Consider how an increase in tax on business profits could affect Mejor Cafe's shareholder dividends and funds available to reinvest. Which effect is likely to be the most important to Mejor Cafe? Justify your answer.

Shareholder dividends:

Funds available to reinvest:

Conclusion: [12]

Total available marks: 80

> BUSINESS FOR CAMBRIDGE IGCSE™ AND O LEVEL: WORKBOOK

WORKED EXAMPLE

Question 1b

Consumers have less income: If consumers have less income, then this is likely to mean that they spend less money [K]. They may buy fewer items such as coffee [Ap]. This will lead to a reduction in sales for Mejor Cafe, which will lead to a reduction in revenue [An]. However, not all products experience a decrease in demand when incomes fall [K]. Some customers may switch to going for a coffee instead of going to a restaurant for a meal out. This could potentially increase sales [An].

Employees might not be as motivated: As tax on people's income has increased, this means that employees earn less money [K]. This could lead to a decrease in motivation. This could cause absenteeism to increase, which would make it harder to offer the same level of service in the cafe [An]. However, some employees might not be motivated by money [K]. They may instead be motivated by factors such as the fact that Major Cafe is an ethical business [Ap]. Therefore, the change in income may not reduce motivation [An].

Conclusion: I think that consumers having less income is likely to have the biggest effect on Mejor Cafe. Consumers are likely to buy more necessity products and less products that they do not necessarily need. Coffee is likely to be something they want rather than something they need. Employees can be motivated by many factors other than money. As they are paid a fair wage already, employees might not become demotivated even if tax on income rises [E].

Improve this answer

This is a sample answer to Case study question 3a. Read through this answer and consider how it could be improved.

Advantage: Consumers have more disposable income [K].

Explanation: This can lead to an increase in demand [An]. Sales for coffee at Mejor Cafe might increase [Ap].

Disadvantage: Difficult to recruit workers as there are less people available to recruit [K].

Explanation: This could mean that Mejor Cafe does not employ the best person for the job [An].

Your challenge

See whether you can improve this answer. This answer has some good parts; there are relevant knowledge points identified in both the advantage and the disadvantage. For advantage 1, there is some good development which shows some analysis, and the answer is written in context of Mejor Cafe. However, there is opportunity to develop the answer further to show additional analysis. Further development of the point is needed. For advantage 2, there is also only one point of analysis. Again, further development is needed. In addition, the second advantage has not been applied to the case study. Try to add relevant context and points of analysis to produce a detailed answer.

> Acknowledgements

The authors and publishers acknowledge the following sources of copyright material and are grateful for the permissions granted. While every effort has been made, it has not always been possible to identify the sources of all the material used, or to trace all copyright holders. If any omissions are brought to our notice, we will be happy to include the appropriate acknowledgements on reprinting.

Thanks to the following for permission to reproduce images:

Cover Image akinbostanci/Getty Images